This slender volume, about the
inspiring, but not in the same v
  It contains no pretty and eas
light beams from heaven. The ins~~~~~~~~~~~~~~~~~~~~~~~
of this country's bloody past and present. The inspiration is there in a
powerful call to action to save our beautiful planet, our children,
grandchildren and loved ones.

—*Frances K. Ransley, author,* This House Protected by Poverty,
2013, Tenacity Press Productions.

Critical Masses is a self-help, non-fiction book, and it assesses the power dynamics and structural inequalities throughout American history. It discusses the system or powers, capitalism, democracy, patriarchy, and so much more.

It was sad to see how the power elite are the ones who control the movement and fate of the living. I found it fascinating to know how schools, churches', propaganda, and strategic positioning affected gender equality, race, and ethnicity. It was evident to see why these topics have always created division amongst people. You can defiantly understand the term divide and conquer when you read this book.

The literature is written well, and it is easy to understand the premise. This is a thought-provoking book, and I enjoyed reading it. I believe books that educate and make you wonder are a great source to have. The subject matter was organized well and presented intriguingly.

—*Jeyran Main, Editor-in-Chief,* Review Tales

Critical Masses diligently examines and challenges global inequality with numerous examples. It is a well-researched piece of work that might be beneficial for those seeking to understand the barriers set forth for certain populations.

—*Mandy Feder Sawyer, Professor, Editor, Journalist*

CRITICAL MASSES

CRITICAL MASSES

WHO WINS
WHO LOSES
WHO DECIDES

JULIE BANKS LEWIS

Critical Masses: Who Wins, Who Loses, Who Decides ©2021
by Julie Banks Lewis

All rights reserved.

LEGAL DISCLAIMER: No part of this book may be reproduced or transmitted in any form or by any means, electronic or mechanical, including photocopying, recording or by any information storage and retrieval system, without written permission from the author. You may not reprint, resell or distribute the contents of this book without express written permission from the author.

First Edition.

Editor: Barbara J. Teel
Managing Editor: Robin Shukle
Design and Production: Liz Mrofka

Cover image by Gorosi.

Printed by: Kindle Direct Publishing

ISBN-13: 979-8463059574

Dedication

To my dear mother, Helen Dorothea Ruth (Heimbach) Fanslow.
8/17/1945 – 2/26/2013

In loving memory of her life and legacy. Thank you for believing that someday I'd do something great for humanity—this is for you Mama!
Love always, Julie

Table of Contents

FOREWORD 10

PREFACE 12

ACKNOWLEDGEMENT 14

INTRODUCTION 15

PART 1
Theory Applied to Lived Experiences and Dominant Historical Narratives

Chapter 1: Agency Vs. Structure 21

Chapter 2: 25
Intersectionality Applied to Public Assistance Beneficiaries

Chapter 3: Dependency, Deviance, and Deservingness ... 29

Chapter 4: 35
It's a [Elite White] Man's World: Civilizational Development and Developmental Citizenship

Chapter 5: 41
Elite White Males and Constructed *Threats* to Civilization

Chapter 6: 47
Colonialization of America: Acculturation, Assimilation, and Annihilation

PART 2
Interlocking Systems of Privilege and Oppression

Chapter 7: Interlocking Systems of Privilege and Oppression 55

PATRIARCHY

Chapter 8: Patriarchy 59

Chapter 9: The Culture of Domination and Violence 65

Chapter 10: 69
Poverty as Violence Against Females and Multiple Oppressions of *Others*

CAPITALISM

Chapter 11: Capitalism 75

Chapter 12: 79
Buying In: Consumerism, Conformance, Commodification, and Consumption

Chapter 13: The Global Power Elite and the Crises of Capitalism......... 85

Chapter 14:... 89
The *Shock Doctrine*: America's Induction Into the Global Capitalist Order

Chapter 15:... 95
The Global Domination Project: Empire Building and Perma-War

DEMOCRACY

Chapter 16: Democracy... 103

Chapter 17: 107
The *Strategy of Tension*: Keeping the Public Pliable and Compliant

Chapter 18:... 113
Ideologies and Institutions: Making Up America's Minds and Capturing Their Hearts

Chapter 19:... 117
American Militarism and Empire: Spreading Democracy or Crushing Rights and Freedoms

Chapter 20:... 123
Belonging Denied: Alienation and Anomie in American Culture

PART 3
Moving Toward a New World Vision

Chapter 21: Speaking Truth to Power: Leveling the Playing Field........ 133

Chapter 22: Changing the Dependency Narrative..................... 137

Chapter 23: Interdependence: The Mutuality of Human Existence...... 141

Chapter 24:... 143
Applications for Social Justice in Policy and Action

Chapter 25:... 147
Multi-Dimensional Oppositional Consciousness: Bridging Divisions and Developing Alliances

Chapter 26: Human Rights: A Framework for Action and Interaction... 151

Conclusion 155

GLOSSARY... 158

ENDNOTES.. 161

BIBLIOGRAPHY... 164

DISUSSION QUESTIONS 170

ABOUT THE AUTHOR.. 172

Foreword

It is with pride and conviction that I write this foreword in solidarity with Julie Lewis. Ms. Lewis appeared at Sonoma State University as a reentering adult from Lake County over 15 years ago with the goal of understanding the sociological underpinnings of being a welfare mom and a powerless culturally dismissed human being. Her journey of consciousness and intellectual maturation are evident in this book. Ms. Lewis recognizes that global inequality, based on race, class and gender, framed the circumstances of her life and that this inequality is maintained by a small class of elites (1%) who have power through the massive control of institutional wealth, power and ideology. She rightfully understands that the 99% of us without wealth, institutional power and police state control have a commonality of self-interest and that we have the power to collectively and individually change the world for the betterment of all.

Julie Lewis's book *Critical Masses* is a timely much needed call for mass collective resistance to the global power elite masters of concentrated wealth and power. Her personal insights, based on her life and circumstances, contribute to the conviction that real revolutionary change is both needed and possible in the world today.

Ms. Lewis is a true human justice resistance fighter using all available resources to build personal and collective settings for positive social change. She recognizes the nature of the forces in power and how their control of governments and media physically and ideologically seek to divide and control the 99%. Yet she knows that the only way forward is the collective undermining of the establishments means of control through ideological consciousness and small resistance actions by millions of people on a daily basis.

Lewis's message is that "we the people" can and will challenge global inequalities in our homes, towns, states and countries using the Universal Declaration of Human Rights as a guiding ideological document for collective agency. Lewis's book informs, encourages, and inspires radical democracy where by important decisions of society are made at the lowest possible level and inviting broad human involvement in building new societies for all.

If a welfare mom from Lake County, California, can write her convictions in this book based on sociological facts and understandings, we cannot be far from providing, "All power to the people" we only need to take the actions step by step to refute global elite inequality.

—Peter Phillips
Sonoma State University: Professor of Sociology

Preface

⚖

The multicultural diversification of the American people with its attendant belief systems, traditions, and contributions is not a 21st Century phenomenon. It is the very fabric of our collective being. Our past is not one history written in a dominant voice as we have been led to believe, but one of countless stories and points-of-view which contribute to the collective makeup and memory of our nation. Those who control the distribution of knowledge, the media-makers and architects of history, have controlled the stories for far too long. The mythologization of the history of this great nation is coming to an end as truths are spoken to power. Voices too long silenced and missing from the annals are emerging in tandem against the status quo and business as usual; in support of a history of the people and a future founded on Truth/truths.

Women, peoples of color, Indigenous, and other marginalized voices are speaking out, telling their truths, offering their stories. Their voices speak to a culture of domination and violence, they speak to empire-building and colonialization. Their stories call out dominant ideologies of whiteness, individualism, homogeneity, heterosexuality, masculinity, and femininity. Their histories are the uncensored versions of what has heretofore been a whitewashed history of the powerful, the conquerors, expansionists, capitalists, and colonialists. The stories of the people are ones of genocide, slavery, assimilation, segregation, and oppression enacted through tools of control.

The true histories expose the lies of empire building and provide a clear understanding of the sacrifices made by the people, often enslaved or indentured in its construction and maintenance. As we gain knowledge, we learn that there are many truths, much more to history, and that what we have been taught and/or allowed to know has been controlled by the dominant groups through media, education, religion, and language. By questioning the dominant narratives and listening to the stories of marginalized peoples, we challenge control of knowledge and insist on a broader understanding; we provide a platform for sharing those experiences which have been distorted by language of the Elite. These suppressed archives of human development, the shared experiences through triumphs and tribulations, and the continued struggles the marginalized face even now—these are the stories of the people. This is the making of America, its' true history from the peoples' perspectives.

This book does not presume to speak for our nation's diverse peoples, nor that the perspectives presented herein are fully representative of oppressed peoples' or marginalized communities' experiences. Rather, historical references will be made throughout the text to demonstrate how power dynamics are implicated in patterns and continuities of interaction dictated by dominant actors and institutions, and how ideologies have been created and manipulated for maintenance of the socio-politico-economic power system and positioning of the population, or status quo.

Acknowledgment

I would like to acknowledge and thank my daughters, Amber Lynne (MacFarland) DuVall, Jacqueline Brooke Hartley, and Taylynn Rae Anne Lewis, my sons-in-laws, Lucas DuVall and Levi Floyd Murray, and my grandson, Jax Julien Michael Murray, for their love, patience, understanding, and unending belief in me during the years-long process of writing this book.

I would like to acknowledge and thank my sister, Belinda Anna Gay Banks-Barnes, for being on my side, for reminding me of my strengths, for holding my hand and holding me up when I faltered, for a lifetime of laughter and hugs, for reminding me that my ideas have value, and that MY voice matters.

I would like to acknowledge and thank my best friend of nearly 30 years, Cynthia Nadine (Koll) Cole, with whom I spent many hours in mind-bending, soul-searching, very human conversations about life, in general, and this book, in particular. Your friendship is priceless.

I would like to acknowledge and thank the unnamed women from Lake County, California, who shared details of their lives as single mothers on welfare. You inspired me with your strength, resilience, fortitude, ingenuity, and capacity for love—to live without limits against all odds.

I would like to acknowledge and thank, Peter Phillips, Author of *Giants: The Global Power Elite,* and Professor of Sociology, Sonoma State University, for caring about your fellow human beings enough to question power and for encouraging others to do the same. I appreciate you for being a source of inspiration, a guide, and a mentor—it has been my honor, sir.

I would like to acknowledge and thank, Robin Shukle and Liz Mrofka of What If? Ideation Business Consulting/Publishing/Design for encouraging me to write this book, for your commitment to helping me see it through to fruition, and for believing in my mission.

Introduction

"Them that's got . . . shall get. Them that's not . . . shall lose. So, the Bible says . . . and it still is news. Mama may have and Papa may have; God Bless the Child, that's got his own." These are the words of a blues song made popular in the 1940s by Billie Holiday. But, what if, as in millions of cases in our great nation, mama does not have and papa's not around? In America today, women account for nearly 70% of people living in poverty, and single mothers are twice as likely as the general population to be rearing their children in desperate circumstances. And, for these mothers now raising their children in poverty the picture doesn't get much brighter as recent studies suggest the greater portion of them even after the children are grown, will continue to be among the nation's poorest citizens. If poverty goes hand in hand with single motherhood, the outstretched fingers are an increased risk of violence and abuse, lack of health insurance and unequal access to health services, inadequate education, lack of childcare, substandard housing, malnutrition, mental health issues, and homelessness.

Historically, the Poor have been marginalized by dominant power structures, and ignorant indifference has led to invisibility. In recent years, there has been a structured attempt to define them out of existence.[1] In shaping public perception and structural concerns, "controlling statistics is a critical function."[2] Statistics are manipulated to minimize poverty, including gross underestimation of the number of poor. Additionally, mainstream media is positioned to create bias against the Poor, depicting *them* as lazy, promiscuous, opportunistic, and criminally deviant. The distinction between *us* and *them* is firmly established as they, many who are single, female heads-of-households who receive public assistance, are blamed for social problems such as increases in crime, drug/alcohol abuse, and juvenile delinquency.

Webster's Dictionary defines poverty as the condition of having little or no money, goods, or means of support; condition of being poor. Social theorists/Sociologists Carl Marx and Max Weber developed the concept of the American stratification system by which societal groups are classified by objective and subjective measures. The objective measure suggested by Marx is based on quantifiable variables such as income and assets. The subjective measures introduced by Weber are based on ways in which we evaluate ourselves and others. Components used to classify individual's socioeconomic position or cultural status include education, occupation, accumulated wealth or assets, and social networks. The combination of economic and social elements allows for large numbers of people to be grouped into socioeconomic classes.

The social rankings of lower, middle, and upper classes have been reconsidered in recent decades such that the upper class is now comprised of an upper-upper class and a lower-upper class. The middle class is now made up of upper-middle, lower-middle, and working class. The working class of the middle and the lower class' working poor share space in barely sustainable or unsustainable wages. While subjective measures may allow individuals to view themselves as part of the middle working class, objective measures would still position these same individuals among the ranks of the lower class or poor.

Individuals and groups upon classification are thus labeled, their place or station inscribed at birth. The class where individuals begin their lives is most often the place where they end. Attempts to move up the socioeconomic ladder of life are moreover dictated by the elite few who occupy the top rung. The people attempting to climb from the lower rungs are members of the middle and working classes. Hanging from the very bottom rung of the ladder are our nation's poor: single mothers and their children, peoples of color, Indigenous, elderly, and disabled. The rungs on the lower half of the ladder have splintered and worn as the ladder has given way under the weight of multiple, entrenched oppressions throughout much of our history. This is of no small consequence; for as we elbow amongst ourselves in efforts to climb the ladder, stepping on fingers and toes, wrestling for an elevated place, scraping and fighting, clinging—the power elites at the pinnacle of this patriarchal ladder are deciding everything for us and benefiting from our collective crises.

We live in a society where power dynamics between the classes, as well as between State and citizen, men and women, whites and *others* are reflected in the socioeconomic positioning of our nation's mass of poor, including Indigenous peoples, people of color, single mothers, elderly, disabled, and young adults. These same dynamics are attendant in interpersonal relations between all humans, and mechanisms for control are maintained by elite structures, institutionalized measures of control, and conventional beliefs and attitudes surrounding being poor, receiving public benefits, or being homeless, which effectively act as society's controls.

This book, a media device, not mainstream-media driven nor corporate-sponsored, is introduced as a counterview, an alternative truth, and public dissent to dominant narratives of American history and human action and interaction. It reveals subjective truths of oppression and repression, marginalization and exclusion, and numerous other markers of eco-socio-political barriers to the full exercise of agency for members of Western society, in general, and the United States, in particular. Expressions of inequities in society are crucial, as without critical analysis of systems of social control/welfare and vociferation by the people, the systems and their masters will continue abetted by conformance, complacency, and complicity.

This book seeks to inform the American public about how power works through the American socio-economic-political systems as illustrated in patterns and continuities of power dynamics throughout history, establish how institutions are created to regulate conformance, compliance, and consumption, demonstrate how ideologies have become institutionalized to support these systems, examine how these systems contribute to beliefs and behaviors, show how stratification and classification systems are used to construct differences for social control, and demonstrate how manipulation of mass consciousness is directed in support of elitist interests.

Additionally, this book is a reconciliatory gesture offered to the millions whose identities are informed by legacies of centuries of racism, sexism, ethnocentrism, and homophobia. In compassion and sympathy for the injustices suffered and lives lost, but especially in solidarity seeking understanding, mercy, and grace in moving forward.

Finally, this book is introduced as part of a global conversation surrounding universal human rights and how the social system of patriarchy, the economic system of capitalism, and faux democracy in Western society are inherently in conflict with these goals. This book is intended to be a unifying device by which people come to understand how the power elites use inner class dynamics based on gender, race, ability, religion, ethnicity, age, and other divisions to keep the people isolated, ill-informed, and paranoid. If enough people understand the social hierarchy that exists in the United States and how the power elite dictate the social, economic, and political directions America is taking, we may raise consciousness to the level of direct action. Until the American people come to know how power works and is wielded to keep people in their place, the elite will continue to win, benefit, decide, and control, while the rest of the "free" world loses. This is of no small consequence of an ignorant or apathetic public, it could quite literally mean that freedom as we have come to understand it will not be a term that applies to the lives we lead, but rather simply part of the rhetoric the empowered use to maintain the status quo.

Until we are all free, we are none of us free.

—E. Lazarus

PART 1

Theory Applied to Lived Experience and Dominant Historical Narratives

CHAPTER 1

Agency vs Structure

*The question I'm always asking myself is:
Are we masters or victims?
Do we make history, or does history make us?
Do we shape the world, or are we just shaped by it?
The question of do we have agency in our lives
or whether we are just passive victims of events is,
I think, a great question.*

—Salman Rushdie

Agency is the human ability to exercise free choice and to act independently of restraints. Restraints on independent action are what are referred to as barriers, and structural barriers are those put in place by societal structures. Structures/systems function through institutions such as religion and education as well as ideologies such as individualism. Institutions and ideologies are manipulated through interlocking power systems: 1) Social—Patriarchy, 2) Economic—Capitalism, and 3) Political—Democratic to create structural barriers to human agency.

Structural barriers to agency effectively limit to varying degrees actions and attitudes of every one of us. Even as we may believe we are making choices free of restraints, we are each constrained by limiting beliefs, our own and those in our environments. Additionally, structures or systems of human interaction have been created for conformance and control, and each of us is born into these systems. Whether we move through these systems/structures with some degree of privilege and ease or are met with multiple oppressions is contingent upon where our birth posits us in terms of categorizations based on gender, race, ethnicity, ability, and other classifications of personhood.

Many might contend that human agency, the ability to exercise free will, counters a structural argument. We each can reason, make choices, decide the outcomes of our decisions, thus, we each ultimately choose whether we will be successful in our endeavors or fail to meet our potential—right? Not quite. Full human agency cannot reasonably be exercised against systems, structures, and institutions of inequality which significantly arrest individual development and development of whole groups of people oppressed by networks of power.

In "Agency and Other Stakes of Poverty," published in *The Journal of Political Philosophy* (2013), Jiwei Ci provides an examination of poverty as relative to the degree to which basic human needs are satisfied by material resources. These needs correspond to types of poverty, or what Ci refers to as the stakes of poverty. The stakes are defined as subsistence or biological needs, status or social needs, and agency or the will to selfhood through power (Ci's definition). Without leveling accusations against modern Western society, Ci provides sufficient evidence that democratic societies face a legitimacy deficit in governance, in failing their responsibility to normal human agency for all their citizens. Indeed, agency is so fundamental a human element that Ci concludes that the worst evil of poverty is its detrimental effect on agency, "the most essential feature of human beings as human beings.[3]"

A striking example of how structural barriers inhibit agency are the masses of Poor, in America and globally. Their exercise of agency is negligible when their powerlessness appears evident. Individuals from the ranks of the poor who have overcome barriers to advancement and achieve what most of their peers do not and likely will not, are the exceptions, not the rule. The rule is found in individual and group socio-eco-political positioning inherent in a patriarchal, capitalist, quasi-democratic society such as the United States of America, whereby our Poor are disenfranchised of rights and privileges held by other American citizens. Further, paradigms of male dominance and white superiority perpetuate systemic sexism and racism, creating and maintaining barriers to inclusion and advancement.

In "Learning from the Outsider Within: The Sociological Significance of Black Feminist Thought," published in *Social Problems* (1986), Patricia Hill Collins states that, "sisterhood is generally understood to mean a supportive feeling of loyalty and attachment to other women stemming from a shared feeling of oppression.[4]" The formed knowledge of members of the sisterhood was at once, from shared experiences of all, and in the unique experience of each. None could separate what they knew, felt, and moved through in current conditions, from what they had lived in their past—it all contributed to their individual consciousness. Each member shared in a feeling of oppression.

The role of parent as the oppressor is played by the paternalistic State as dictated by Elite white males, the insiders. Black feminist thought argues that a significant factor shaping consciousness of their oppression is "their experience at the intersection of multiple structures of domination.[5]" Black women, the sisterhood of outsiders are simultaneously oppressed by racism and sexism (by insiders). Additionally, individual members may experience discrimination associated with disabilities, poverty, or exhibiting "deviant behavior" in sexual orientation or identity. They are truly outsiders within a society of insiders.

In understanding the social dynamics within and outside, Black Feminist thought offers a broader understanding of the pivot point on the matrix of oppression from which black women form consciousness. Activity performed upon recognition of oppression by the conscious mind is summed up well by Collins when she states, "self-definition and self-valuation are not luxuries—they are necessary for Black female survival."[6] Black feminist literature leaves little doubt of the truth in that statement as their shared stories illustrate the creativity of these women in finding everyday ways of coping and moving on.

Finally, when Collins speaks to the issue of incorporating Black Feminist thought into traditional sociology as well as other disciplinary practices, she suggests "conserving the creative tension of the outsider within status"[7] in seeing things in a new way. The new way is a" humanist vision —the freedom both to be different and to be part of the solidarity of humanity."[8] I believe this applies to the multiple accounts of history which are now offering us fuller insights into the development of America. We all might benefit from seeing things from the outside in.

For the hundreds of millions living within the confines of poverty, their experiences are profoundly affected by their socioeconomic position. Institutions and societal controls act to limit these people's agency through external measures, and the Poor internalize societal beliefs and associated stigma which effectively act to inhibit action. However, the lived experiences revealed in personal narratives of welfare recipients in Lake County, California, and in alternative histories of marginalized and oppressed people around the world attest to strength, resilience, fortitude, and determination in overcoming structural barriers and in exercising agency.

CHAPTER 2

Intersectionality Applied to Public Assistance Beneficiaries

"Intersectionality draws attention to invisibilities that exist in feminism, in anti-racism, in class politics, so, obviously, it takes a lot of work to consistently challenge ourselves to be attentive to aspects of power that we don't ourselves experience."

—Kimberle' Williams Crenshaw

Essential to an understanding of members of the Poor and their barriers to exercise of agency is a theoretical framework of intersectionality. The framework utilized here provides a cohesive understanding of the multidimensional oppressions experienced by individuals and groups bound by interlocking systems of power made manifest in American patriarchy, capitalism, and a barely functioning democracy. Additionally, the framework allows for connections to be made between structure and agency, and how power dynamics operate for construction of classifications, control and punishment of populations, and maintenance of the status quo.

Welfare recipients, as members of the Poor, are simultaneously expected to meet standards of conformance yet, restricted in access to life's fundamental needs. For single mothers, especially those who receive public assistance, inequalities of condition and opportunity are lived realities for them and their children. Intersectionality theorists argue that, "oppression is produced through the interaction of multiple, decentered, and co-constitutive axes."[9] Theirs is a place of multiple societal oppressions, many invisible, designed for control and punishment—for being women, for being out-of-wedlock with children, for being poor, and for not measuring up to society's demands for self-sufficiency.

Concepts of gender, class, and race divide and separate these women from American society, in this case, a small rural community in Northern California. Though the women studied come from a place of privilege as members of the white race, gender and class combine to marginalize them as outsiders within. In actions, even as they strive for middle class standards in their lives, their low socioeconomic status allows for prejudice and judgment as labels of poor white trash, hick, and trailer trash are applied to them by community members, especially, administrators and workers in the welfare offices.

Patriarchal bargaining enables these women to identify themselves at a more elevated place than members of their same economic class via the same cultural divisions adhered to in larger society. It is precisely because racism is accepted in American society, that it is perpetuated. Thus, they may with social impunity, assess others who are Black, Latino, or Native American, as of lower status than themselves. Further, in attempts to distance themselves from welfare mothers who are assumedly, undeserving, because of alcoholism or drug addiction, sexual orientation, or have numerous sexual partners, the women apply stereotypes and labels to each other.

Contempt is not limited to these women's low economic status; they are further scorned as husbandless women with illegitimate children. Dichotomies of virgin and whore are not reserved to those who would pass moral judgment on these women's lives. They mark out boundaries for inclusion or exclusion in everyday lived experiences. Making choices to have children as unmarried women, especially when they lack income or resources to adequately support them, leaves these women as targets of disdain and contempt.

These women are perceived as shunning conventional rules for women's roles and acceptable behaviors, thus, they effectively, if unknowingly, set themselves up for compartmentalization and ridicule. Edicts of welfare policy, especially as applied to cash aid recipients, require cooperation with child support services, which entails the sharing of intimate details relative to sexual activity. No reasonable expectation for privacy is allowed as these women must answer questions about who they have had sex with, how many times, for how long, how many partners they have had, and do they have witnesses to substantiate their answers. If they try to evade these personal invasions, they are sanctioned for non-cooperation and denied assistance.

Capitalism combines with patriarchy in defining these women's situated positions in larger society. The ideology of individualism that pervades America, mandates participation in the marketplace and responsibility for being self-supporting. Though they work, often more than one job, they do not earn enough to sustain their families, and so they must depend on public assistance to make ends meet. Because they are not self-sufficient, they are considered needy and dependent; essentially identified as takers, their contributions, if considered at all, are valueless and they, unworthy.

Contrary to notions of equality, the American political system is but a vestige of democratic society, whereby inequities and injustices suffered by marginalized citizens have become standard. Subjugated members of society, single welfare mothers of Lake County, California, and millions of other Poor are constitutive parts of an underclass of citizens whose lives are caught up in a quagmire of oppression. The concurrent effects of being women, having children without benefit of marriage, and of being on the lowest end of the economic spectrum, position these women outside of normative societal boundaries. Belongingness may never be realized by these women, their children, or millions of others in the lowest income bracket. Economic mobility for them is experienced in mostly lateral moves along a horizontal playing field. Realization of upward mobility is an expectation not grounded in lived experience.

Interlocking systems of patriarchy, capitalism, and democracy allow the Elite to manipulate power dynamics to their advantage and to the decided disadvantage of the masses. Hierarchal classifications posit members of society as privileged or oppressed, a combination of both, or as is too often the case, suffering multiple, intersecting oppressions simultaneously. And, while white people, moreover, are privileged by the lack of melanin in their skin as even poor whites move about in society with relative ease in contrast to movements by peoples of color and Indigenous peoples; patterns and continuities in American history demonstrate poor whites too, have been and continue to be subject to prejudicial treatment and discrimination. Though they are white, they are poor which is a marker of deficiency in moral code and/or character, deviant in their inability to meet self-reliance goals, and often dependent, thus they are simultaneously marked for exclusion and control. These marginalized groups are born into a society that has already classified them by their socioeconomic status and/or by the color of their skin as undeserving and a threat to be controlled and punished. Individual and group agency is barred by institutional sexism, racism, ageism, ableism, and numerous other socially constructed differences created and maintained to keep marginalized individuals and whole groups of *others* where Elites decide they should be and where control may be maintained.

CHAPTER 3

Dependency, Deviance, & Deservingness

"Deserve was such a strange word, throwing out both blame and accolades with equal mercilessness. Society's skewed scale for assigning a value to human beings. How many times had he been judged and found lacking? Was there ever a way to measure what anyone deserved?"

—Sonali Dev

A framework of intersectionality applied to the lives of single welfare mothers in Lake County, California, and more broadly to members of the Poor, can be understood within the confines of the interlocking systems of patriarchy, capitalism, faux democracy, and attendant institutionalized conceptualizations of gender, race, and class.

Applying these analyses to single mothers who receive public assistance finds these women are compartmentalized as dependent, excluded for deviance, and granted only provisional citizenship. Provisional citizenship allows for them to receive public benefit, but they are simultaneously subject to infringement upon their rights as the implied understanding of receipt restricts any expectance of privacy. As dependents, they are deviant; as deviants they are threats; and finally, as threats they must be controlled.

Dominant American ideologies of individualism and self-sufficiency define and instruct differentials of power in class, gender, and racially based interactions. Ideologies have been institutionalized over time and are implicated in the subjugation of women and marginalized peoples. Thus, people's lives are constructed as patterned by and arranged relative to, gender, sexuality, class, and race. Markers of belonging or exclusion are operative within these parameters and position single mothers receiving welfare benefits and other members of the Poor as undeserving.

Stratification is not limited to socioeconomic class, but further applied to the status of being poor, especially regarding dependence, as the Poor are divided into the deserving or entitled, and those who are undeserving. While the term, deserving poor, may be interpreted as an oxymoron, there is now and has historically been a debate surrounding divisions based on worth and merit. Definitions of deserving as applied, mean that an individual is worthy, held in esteem, merits respect, or is held in high regard. However, poverty does not posit any member of the poor, thusly. Moreover, our society holds individuals to a standard of conformity, which includes a personal responsibility, even a moral obligation, to be self-supporting. Indeed, if an individual fails to conform to the standard, she is held to be deficient, and further, blameworthy whereby the responsibility for her condition is assigned to her.

Individualism is our American ethos; it pervades American consciousness and promotes values of independence and self-reliance, while vilifying dependence. Further, patterns and continuities throughout American history speak to ways in which public consciousness has been manipulated to acceptance of paradigms of whiteness and white supremacy as well as, normative ideals of masculinity, femininity, and heterosexuality. The intersection of these paradigms and ideologies contributes to power relations structured in social and economic classifications, whereby the Elite decide, control, and benefit while masses of Poor struggle to survive while shouldering the blame for society's ills.

The dominant dependency narrative posits these women as un-American in failing to meet their responsibility to the individualist ideal and obligation to be self-supporting. Further, moral implications promote controlling images of welfare mothers as lazy and opportunistic. Dependence is constructed in contrast to ideals of self-sufficiency such that deficiencies in behavior, prescribed by dominant societal narratives, are considered deviant. This deviance from normative ideals is associated with negative attributes and threats, and further, pathologized in medicalized understanding such that dependency is presented as deficiencies of development. Thus, dependency becomes an illness for which society must prescribe a cure.

This dependency narrative is applied to international relationships as well, especially debtor nations and their people, against whom austerity measures are enacted, effectively eliminating public support programs and increasing policing efforts. The leaders of these nations and by extension, the citizens, are penalized for not meeting their financial obligations in repayment of loans. It is the people, however, who are punished in abject poverty and control of their persons, they have no realistic expectation of betterment of condition. They lack food, shelter, access to clean water, and sanitation, the bare necessities for life.

Controls and institutionalized measures, both capitalist and patriarchal, which create and maintain the dominant culture as dictated by civilized, propertied, white men's control of dependent members of society, here and abroad, are introduced in restrictive welfare measures, some behavioral and others economic. Modern interpretations posit single, female, heads-of-households who receive public assistance as threats to an ordered society, thus controls were instituted in the Personal Responsibility and Work Opportunity Reconciliation Act (PRWORA) of 1996 as welfare reform. The act as prescriptive design to pathological dependence,[10] required recipients of public aid to conform to work requirements and limited entitlements of benefits to five years, with the California state limits set at 48 months.

In "Of Witches, Welfare Queens, and the Disaster Named Poverty: The Search for a Counter-Narrative," published in the Journal of Poverty, Shawn A. Cassiman (2006) explores the origins of the dependency narrative and construction of the "welfare queen" in poverty policy, examines how social work has contributed to the narrative, and discusses how a counter-narrative organized within a trauma paradigm might be advanced. Her method is a review of social work and social science textbooks in which she reviews the dominancy of the dependency narrative and how focus on professionalization in social work contributes to the dominant narrative. She contends that identification of deviant populations, such as dependents, serves dual purposes of reinforcing social norms and isolating the deviant.[11] Additionally, she demonstrates how dependency as deviance, has been internalized by society as negative, indeed, in development of the dominant dependent/deviant narrative, concepts of mutual dependency and interdependence, and understandings of their "value of care" are ignored.[12] Further, she provides a discussion on the historical nature of the dependency narrative as a continuation of the pauper discourse found in colonial America,[13] whereby paupers as dependents were marked as deviant relative to the normative individual who was industrious and godly, thus as just reward accumulated wealth. The pauper, was then, as the Poor are now, associated with a lack of industry or laziness and deviant behaviors including licentiousness. As juxtaposed to American ideals of individualism and self-sufficiency, the un-American dependency/deviancy narrative has been developed into a medicalization and pathologization of poverty.

Institutional controls in the form of dominant ideologies, act to suppress agency as based on an invisible authority. Community members' prejudices, beliefs, and attitudes surrounding welfare mothers effectively limit attempts to exercise agency through associated stigma. Prevailing notions of worth are embedded in conceptualizations of single, female, heads of households who receive public assistance. Representations of welfare mothers by mainstream media fuel misperceptions and prejudices in American culture contributing to their continued marginalization and powerlessness. Internalizing these preconceptions, these women become stigmatized by society and doubt their own worth as they heap blame and shame on themselves. Conversely, to elevate themselves relative to other mothers who receive welfare, they apply comparative measures whereby, they inflate other's failings, whilst indicating how they act to meet conformance standards.

Continuity as applied to the construction of womanhood has been inextricably linked to construction of the *other* in terms of racism and classism; all in continued response to a patriarchal, capitalist structured society. Each person constructs conceptual distinctions in creating social boundaries on the cognitive, interactive, and institutional levels. Thus, boundary work is a fundamental function of identifying self and others, not only relative to living within the ecopolitical confines of the State, but in comparison across international divides, as well. This is where the concept of patriarchal bargaining comes into play, as we each try to find our place on the hierarchal pyramid. With the politics of domination contributing to increased nationalism and racialization, restructuring of class relations, and the transformation of family lives inherent in globalization; we are each doing our own patriarchal bargaining. But the bargaining position seems to be lateral for most of the people with vertical movement more often occurring downward rather than up, as we are conditioned to believe by corporate media espousing the ideologies of the free-market system, domestically and internationally.

Even women positioned in a privileged place operate under the constructs of patriarchy as they bargain in lateral steps for power that is leveled by a glass ceiling. The playing field is not level for all players, and thus, we bargain. And, in that bargaining we mark out boundaries; boundaries that give us advantage, boundaries that protect us, and boundaries that divide and separate us. These boundaries work to the benefit of the Power Elite, obscuring the vision of the people and inhibiting opportunities for working together toward common goals for all of humanity. Boundaries matter. As long as boundaries divide individuals and groups along gender, race, and class lines, the structural mechanism that drives the capitalist machine will continue to be oiled by the blood, sweat, and tears of the ever-increasing, never-deserving Global Poor.

Paradigms of whiteness, masculinity, femininity, and heterosexuality inscribe meaning for ways of being and moving about in Western society. They provide normative schemas for all members to follow within the confines of patriarchy, capitalism, and democracy of/for the Elite. We are each, male and female, black and white, young, and old, indoctrinated into the system and dogma embedded through media, education, religion, and culture toward goals of assimilation, acculturation, and homogeneity of the masses, and hegemony for white, elite males. Non-normative role-breakers and rule-breakers, nonconformists to forced ideals in Americanized culture find their differences are perceived and presented as deviant with negative connotations implied. Their deviance often positions them as dependent; their inability to meet individualist goals of self-reliance, marking them for further exclusion and control by the dominant power structures. They are classified as takers, drains, and threats by the dominant power players; thus, prejudice and judgment may be applied marking them as undeserving of compassion and empathy, not worthy of basic human kindness, nor treatment with respect and dignity.

CHAPTER 4

It's A [Elite White] Man's World: Civilizational Development and Developmental Citizenship

"Plainly put, the imperative to "be professional" [normative model] is the imperative to be whiter, straighter, wealthier, and more masculine. A wolf in sheep's clothing masquerading as a neutral term, professionalism [normal] hangs over the head of anyone who's different, who deviates from the hegemony of white men."

— Jacob Tobia

Relationships and citizen participation are manipulated within the parallel trajectories of civilizational and human development. Thus, presented herein is a multi-layered conversation on civilizational development and developmental citizenship which includes all the overlapping and linking aspects implied in hierarchal classification systems such as exist in American society. This discussion is developed premised on the notion of the United States of America as the epitome of civilization. Further, that the potential for civilization is realized in the development of the human subject as embodied in the white, heterosexual, able bodied, propertied, American man (normative subject). Additionally, the potential for civilization is related to the normative subject's manipulation of relationship patterns with women and other men, which are indicative of others perceived contribution or threat to civilization. These relationships are internal to larger processes of exclusion and inclusion operating relative to access to the body politic. Thus, categorizations of race, gender, ability, class, age, etc. reflect social positioning and control in developmental citizenship for maintenance of and control by the Power Elite.

Belonging, compartmentalization, and exclusion are determined as implicit to an individual's position (evolution) along the civilizational/human development trajectory. Belonging is implied for the normative subject as full citizen of the United States with all the rights and privileges inherent. From this place, the pinnacle of society, he determines where all others are situated. Historically, woman has been positioned as subordinate to man. Keeping with hetero-patriarchal, capitalist notions, woman's status is determined relative to the normative subject in her reproductive capacity and her contribution to his labor power. [He] owns her contributions and thus, may control her, her function, and realize any benefit of her participatory efforts. Gender, then, is central to this or any discussion of power; as is the construction of roles, expectations, definitions, etc. as cultural societal controls.

Civilization operates for the normative subject and for his continued domination and evolution. The product of the assumed heterosexual male and female relationship is progeny. Children, especially males, represent continuation of the species and moreover, further human/civilizational development toward the goal of a super-man. Further, the heterosexual couple has a responsibility to society of fertility. By extension, society (as an imperialist nation) assumes the right to foster and expand life or alternately to deny and decimate lives as exercises of sovereign power and to limit and control undesirable population growth.

As a patriarchal society, where value is concentrated in and perpetuated through the male, a woman's role has historically been valued in reproductive terms. The woman's worth is valued in terms of reproductive capacity, thus those women who conceive outside of a nuptial arrangement are acting against normative boundaries, diminishing their worth by society's standards. Children born of these women are illegitimate, or bastard children, thus not supported within an acceptable patriarchal union, nor considered by the dominant society as worthy or deserving. These cultural scripts enable stratification based on gender, race, sexuality, ability, and age as indicated in a hetero-patriarchal, capitalist system of structuring. The benefits of citizenship are all to be realized by the Elite white man as normative model and his dominance over women, children, and perceived *others*, as they in turn are excluded from full participation in society.

In preserving rights of citizenship and civilization, the normative subject supported by society must be ever mindful of threats to civilization, moreover, to maintaining the status quo. These threats are often presented as degrees of difference from the normative subject. These distinctions based on gender, race, sexuality, class, religion, etc. are created in determining assimilability or belongingness into the dominant culture. Unmet assimilation is countered in measures to isolate and confine individuals and entire populations, as seen with tribes of Indigenous peoples re-located to reservations, as well as, in the ghettoization of peoples of color, and the build-up of the prison-industrial-complex.

Scientific racism and medicalization of human activity are tools that have been used historically to construct categories of distinction and difference. Society institutionalizes patterns of inclusion/exclusion as measures for preservation of civilization, and society members internalize beliefs and attitudes against perceived *others*. These methods are social controls operating at the community level and beyond, as determined in legislative measures and judicial commitments. Beyond the level of sanction for deviation from the norm on an individual basis, laws have been created to manipulate and control entire groups of *others*.

The social construction of categories of race, gender, class, sexuality, and ability or disability situate individuals and groups for participation in larger society. Full citizens (normative model) are granted full participation, rights, access to benefits, and control of resources. Provisional citizenship allows for restricted participation in society with limited access to benefits, situational rights, and control of the individual as a reproductive or labor resource. Provisional citizenship provides for compartmentalization of individuals and groups based on perceived contribution to society and assimilability into the dominant culture. Exclusion suggests lack of contribution, unassimilable character/culture, and/or a threat or menace to society. These individuals and groups, as implied, are excluded from participation as full citizens of this nation and are entitled to little benefit or rights. Compartmentalization and exclusion are manipulated in social construction and control measures, often interchangeably and simultaneously.

The politics of power in social construction vary according to social activity of the players and the interests of the controlling party. The model subject maintains his position along the civilizational/human development trajectory in the subordination of others, here again, supported by the state in military exercises, legislation, and ideological persuasions or nationalistic ideologies. The ideological network is not confined to the religious, as can be readily identified in groups of people believing and acting on ideologies which are also cultural and political, e.g., political associations, sports, and gangs.

Curiously, man's (normative subject) evolutionary potential is yet to be realized. Discourse on developmental citizenship suggests that there is a parallel trajectory between human development and civilization. While it can be illustrated (to some degree) that the model subject is moving along this trajectory; historical archives, as well as, current national and international events, present evidence of significant deviations in moving toward a civilized society. Definitions of the word civilized include its use as an adjective denoting an advanced and humane culture/society. We are, indeed, an advanced society, leaders in technology and scientific endeavors. However, this meaning obscures the additional term, humane; characterized by tenderness, compassion, and sympathy for other beings, especially for the suffering or distressed.

If civilization is to run parallel to human development, then the normative subject must incorporate humane measures into personal and public interactions, and additionally, place humanity at the pinnacle of civilization. Race, gender, age, ability, and class as socially constructed categories used to determine individual's and groups' rights to citizenship and access to participation in civilized society, need to be reconstructed for inclusion on equal terms. Civilization cannot reasonably stand on a broken foundation, nor can it be built with missing pieces. The foundation and the building blocks are found in humanity. For civilization to advance, for human beings to truly evolve, participation can no longer be determined in terms of developmental citizenship. We must go beyond conceptualizing distinctions between us and *others* as acceptable in creating boundaries, and base our understanding in concrete terms. Terms grounded in cooperation, not competition, in fulfilling human needs and protecting and healing the earth, not terms structured by profit and control.

CHAPTER 5

Elite White Males and Constructed *Threats* to Civilization

"If you look at great human civilizations, from the Roman Empire to the Soviet Union, you will see that most do not fail simply due to external threats but because of internal weakness, corruption, or a failure to manifest the values and ideals they espouse."

—Corey Booker

American Modernity contains the essential elements for the development of civilization. These elements are: 1) Political—practical extension of rights and/or the restrictions put upon them in developmental citizenship (consider the extension of the right to vote to the Black man and the methods used to then disenfranchise him), 2) Economic—elements are considered against the Industrial Revolution in the development of mass corporations which controlled labor, laws, and rights, as well as, explosion of bureaucracies, and 3) Socio-Cultural—aspects of belonging, provisional access, and exclusion as positioned against continuation of the dominant (superiority implied) white race.

Patterns and continuities for the advancement of the white male are evident throughout American history as seen in the subjugation of women and people of color. For the Elite white male, continued development was viewed as dependent on avoidance of arrested development (Negro rapist), avoidance of degeneration of the white race through muddying of the genetic pool (feeble-minded), and avoidance of becoming overly civilized (referred to as neurasthenia/neurasthenic man).

Provisional access provides for compartmentalization and exclusion of individuals and whole groups of people. This compartmentalization and/or exclusion (they can occur separately or simultaneously) is developed against a *threat* to society, the dominant race, and civilization itself. In compartmentalizing or excluding, positioning can be established for access to rights and privileges within the dominant society. However, perceived threats must be dealt with, and methods have been developed by American culture throughout history to penalize actors outside of the *norm*.

Three of the threats, dangerous figures, posed to civilization within American Modernity are the Negro rapist, the feeble-minded, and the neurasthenic man. The Negro rapist was constructed as a threat to civilization in that it posed a threat to white women's virtue, thereby inviting society as an extension of white, civilized men, to step into the chivalrous role as protector. The Negro rapist was dynamically positioned as opposite to white, civilized manhood as primitive, savage, and prone to acting out aggressively, sexually and otherwise. The deeper concern of the dominant culture was to segregate members of society by distinctions of race, illustrated in distance from the white ideal, for maintaining white superiority. In this instance race as constructed, offered this distance. The distance was enforced and barriers fortified through legislation, creating laws intended to keep *others* at a distance; in schools, public arenas, and housing. Additionally, and importantly, differences were amplified to elevate white men and subjugate Blacks socially, economically, and politically. The dehumanization of Blacks, in general, men in particular, allowed for, even encouraged mistreatment and persecution by public authorities and private citizens alike.

Scientific racism and medicalized nativism and by extension medicalized racism are evident as continuities in Elitist agendas to maintain white supremacy and subjugation of all *others*. With the advent of eugenics as the new scientific method of the period, yet another stratification was made possible. Wherein, traits were passed on through generations by biological factors, it stood to reason that defective traits could be lessened in occurrence and severity by controlling reproduction by individuals of degenerate groups. In "Three Generations of Imbeciles Are Enough," Matt Wray traces the methods of social Darwinism "to rationalize and legitimize social inequalities and hierarchies of domination.[14]" Poor, white, rural degenerates were found to be deficient, thus following recapitulation theory generation after generation would continue to be deficient, each perhaps more so even than the last. Further, to avoid degeneration of the White race, the Poor, who were considered both socially deficient and behaviorally deviant, could not be allowed to procreate. Thus, Poor women, White, Black, Brown, and Indigenous were constructed as threats to development of the white race and to civilization, itself. IQ testing was introduced to effectively abate the concerns of public burden, lack of labor contribution, and degeneration of the race based on intellect. Individuals whether mentally deficient in any capacity or not, if Poor, were classified as feeble-minded and institutionalized to contain them at a distance from larger society. Grouped into the feeble-minded category for degenerates, they were systematically sterilized to prevent introduction of inferior stock to the gene pool. The label of and classification as feeble-minded was widely interpreted and applied to members of the poor, especially females. In fact, the landmark case Buck v. Bell (1927), Justice Oliver Wendell Holmes Jr. declared that "three generations of imbeciles were enough" and adjudicated that those residents who were designated as being feebleminded or socially inadequate could be sterilized against their will as prevention of risk for continuation of degenerate or deficient offspring. The case legitimized State governments' power as more than 70,000 Poor women were sterilized against their wills; the very last of these injustices having been performed in 1981.

The third threat to civilization is the overly civilized or neurasthenic man (civilized and White implied). In trying to keep pace with modern civilization, the neurasthenic man presents as weary, weak, degenerate, and often effeminate. Obviously, civilization cannot continue to develop and advance if its chief players are sidelined for over-indulgence in self-control measures, thus the paradox of neurasthenia. In "Teaching Our Sons to Do What We Have Been Teaching the Savages to Avoid: G. Stanley Hall, Racial Recapitulation, and the Neurasthenic Paradox", Gail Bederman profiles G. Stanley Hall, a renowned pedagogist/educator of the late 19th Century and analyzes his manipulation of racial recapitulation in the 1880s to address the neurasthenic paradox faced by white, civilized men.

In offering up a method for abating the problem, Hall argued that white males "highly evolved" bodies had been physically weakened by their "nerve force" being depleted by modern civilization. Thus, manly restraint became a cultural weakness defined in medical terms as neurasthenia; neurasthenic men were essentially ill due to strict adherence to self-control measures as necessitated in development of civilized man and by extension, civilization. Hall contended that white adolescent males were at the same level of development as adults of primitive races. And, while white boys could be "inoculated" through education to eventually fulfill their "super-man" destinies, adolescent/primitive races suffered arrested development and could never be fully developed or civilized men. Thus, white boys, as young white males should be encouraged to actively promote their primitive natures in physically aggressive ways.

Hall argued the remedy to neurasthenia was to encourage "boys to be boys," promoting violence and hyper-activity as "natural" to the young white male and by which adult males might retain some primitive aspect of themselves. Then, in adolescence the males should be highly educated to promote transition into manhood. Curiously, if girls received excessive education, it could damage their reproductive systems, leaving them sterile. Even grown women, then, could never be truly developed, nor civilized. Truly, only adolescent white boys held the future of the developing world in their hands. This ridiculous scenario and legitimization for developing a masculine man still plays out in contemporary times. Hall's pedagogy was widely subscribed to and his methods utilized until eugenics provided that hereditary was biologically linked to chromosomes, not recapitulation from generations passed. The meanings of masculinity, and the markers of maleness and manhood, contribute to acceptance of violence as part of a male's natural makeup, and aggressiveness is suggestive of males, especially white men's, right to dominate.

Though the era of modernity has passed, the end of the 20th century and the first two decades of the twenty-first century have seen a resurgence in nativism and ethnocentrism. Questions of how race, class, and gender shaped early 20th C. medicine and immigration policies are examined in "Medicalizing the Mexican: Immigration, Race, and Disability in the Early-20th Century United States", by Natalia Molina. Molina illustrates how the construction of the racial category "Mexican" was developed around the physical body of Mexican immigrant workers and their kinship networks. Developed in capitalist terms, Mexican suggested a special affinity to manual labor, subordinate and docile and as immigrant workers, "birds of passage,[15]" unlikely to stay too long and be a drain on society. And, of paramount importance to capitalists, Mexican immigrant workers were a "source of low-skill, low-wage labor." Further, Molina provides an analysis of how U.S. immigration policies were both shaped by, and contributed to, racial and ability-based classifications for citizenship. In 1916 during the Typhus Fever outbreak, the category was developed to suggest *Mexican* as "racially inferior, inherently less able-bodied, and more prone to infection and to be infectious,[16]" thereby, simultaneously depicting the *Mexican* as dangerous and a drain on society. Additionally, the threat of Mexican American "children citizens"[17] controlling national soil contributed to an even more degenerate construction of the category. Immigration policies were adjusted to screen for good laborers and those fit to be citizens in consideration of capitalist goals and nationalist goals. Mexicans were simultaneously compartmentalized as suitable laborers yet excluded as citizens.

As evidenced herein, medicalized nativism and scientific racism have been applied to scientific inquiries with resultant terms applied for classification and stratification of groups of people. These tools have historically been used to rationalize and legitimize social inequalities and hierarchies of domination in support of white superiority and dominance. More recent interpretations can be readily applied to the disproportional infection and mortality rates of COVID-19 on the Poor, including Black, Latino, and Indigenous populations; this in large part due to lack of access to and continuity of care. The power of science to contribute to social perceptions and attitudes and to label behaviors can still be used to develop human solidarity and unity but must be applied to those ends. An ethics of care, contrary to historical interventions by the Elite, needs to be applied, as they [Power Elite] continue to exercise decisions of life and death, of quality of lives, and access to basic needs for all American citizens.

Historical patterns and continuities in Elite domination demonstrate a devaluing of womanhood, of racial diversity, of disability, of the poor, of youth, and of the aged. Elite white males have created a patriarchal, capitalist, faux democratic world; one in which they decide the conditions of being for all peoples based on benefit to themselves. Indeed, they have manipulated science, religion, ideologies, and institutions with utter disregard for the human condition and the sustainability of life on this planet. They fear Blacks and other people of color, they fear women, they fear homosexuals and gender nonconformists. They fear critical masses, they fear unity and solidarity of the people, they fear collective action (unless it aligns with their goals), they fear change to the status quo. They fear what they do not understand, yet, understanding would necessitate caring consideration of *others*; of *others'* needs, expectations, desires, hopes, and fears. Paradoxically, the Elite's collective fears of *others* have created the very conditions which disallow a civilized society.

CHAPTER 6

⚖

Colonialization of America: Acculturation, Assimilation, And Annihilation

"The great lie is that it is civilization. It's not civilized. It has been literally the most bloodthirsty brutalizing system ever imposed upon this planet. That is not civilization. That's the great lie, is that it represents civilization."

—John Trudell

Exceptionalism has been written into dominant historical narratives to such an extent that much of what the public learns of history has been based in hero-worship and celebration of conquest and expansion. Exceptionalism in American consciousness has moreover been reserved for the winners of wars, actual and ideological. These exceptional men, the conquerors, capitalists, and colonialists are written into the pages of history for public adulation and reverence. The crimes committed against humanity for the sake of capital growth are conveniently absent from discourse or contextualized as necessary and for the benefit of the people conquered. The stories have been repeated so often that myths and legends have been created. This is the mythologization of history, the construction in written form of superior white men's tales of glory, of predestiny, and of paternalism—our national memories manipulated and managed in support of imperialist goals.

In challenging the history we have been taught, and further in subjecting official narratives throughout time to critical analysis, the power dynamics are elucidated, the modus operandi of the decision makers in setting the goals and vetting the gains in/of conflict are made clear. Most significantly, history must be subjected to truths from *others*, women, Indigenous peoples, peoples of color—the subordinated and subjugated, the conquered and colonized, the oppressed, and the resistors to empire.

American history has been manipulated to enforce dominant doctrines of white supremacy, individualism, and unfettered capitalism. Homogeneity in a patriarchal society insists that all members conform to normative scripts and comply with rules for being and moving about. This homogeneity is relative to individual and group identities, differences in culture, religion, tradition, etc., often being subsumed by the dominant culture. The dominant culture masters of the United States have historically been white, heteronormative, propertied, and Christian. Additionally, establishment of this nation was motivated by the interests of early capitalists for maintenance of position and property.

In *Changes in the Land: Indians, Colonists, and the Ecology of New England,* by William Cronon, cultural differences in land use are understood to have substantially impacted early colonialists' interactions with both the land and those who inhabited it. The Europeans' conceptions of "property, wealth, and boundaries on the landscape"[18] contributed to early America's first clash of cultures. While the Indigenous peoples tended to have a spiritual connection to the land and nature, colonialists' connection was a material one as the only connectivity was one of monetary value. Thus, the commodification of the land and "things that were on the land"[19] has created a relationship by which degradation of the earth and depletion of natural resources has occurred.

Cronon suggests European (white males) perceptions of Indian males as lazy savages were informed by local indigenous' reliance on hunting and fishing, which Europeans considered leisure activities. In Europeans' view, Indian women who planted and raised the crops, much like Colonial men did, were the only productive members of tribal people[20]. Further, "failure of the Indians to adequately subdue the soil as Genesis 1:28 required,"[21] justified the colonists/conquerors in claiming the land, indifferent to any claims of "sovereignty"[22] by the native peoples. This subduing of the soil necessarily included inclosing/enclosing the land and "improving"[23] it—a way of life with which the European colonists were familiar. Theirs was a lifestyle which required permanence, as in permanent structures and cleared and cultivated fields for planting and raising domesticated animals. Thus, the native plants and animals which first inhabited the New England countryside were dealt with in much the same manner as the native people were treated, cut down and cleared from the land. In the colonialists' minds, the bounty of the new country was infinite, and the land was theirs for the taking. Meanings of property and the proper use of land as well as, influence from the market in early capitalist America contributed substantially to waste of natural resources, extinction of wild animals, changes in the soil, climate, water variables, and numerous other ecological effects.

The market helped to establish those things of the land which could be used as commodities, as well as imbuing the land itself with value, especially when subdued and put to productive use and improvements made upon it. A white man could accumulate wealth/capital, simply through private land (property) ownership, but the idea was to build capital. Scarcity of various materials in England, as well as desire for such status items as furs, helped to develop a market for American resources and early-American-made goods. Taxes imposed on landowners, especially farmers, forced many into the marketplace where the accumulation of surplus goods became a necessity to acquire materials[24]. Many of the resources of the land were laid to waste in favor of other more marketable items. Furbearing animals and lumber were key commodities and their consumption led to extinction of species. Methods for clearing the land for purposes of improvement or increased capital had deleterious ecological results. Flooding, soil deterioration, increased disease, and other effects could be traced to capital's influence on the way colonists made use of the land and lived in their environment.

In the colonializing process, appropriation of land and resources and the dispossession of Indigenous populations are key elements. Colonialists viewed the land as a place to conquer, claim, and extract all the valuable resources from. These views were given merit in the informal adoption of the doctrine of Manifest Destiny. It was believed that it was ordained by God that the people of the young republic should expand white civilization across the country. This notion in varied form has been used as justification in modern times for America's imperialist ambitions in the global arena. Relationships between white colonialists and the Indigenous peoples have historically been influenced by patriarchy vis-a`-vis white superiority, Christianity, and capitalism.

Cultural institutions of religion and public education have historically been employed as tools for acculturation. Public institutions of compulsory education and dominant religious influences were instrumental in attempts to acculturate Native Americans for assimilation into American society. Once the Indigenous had been conquered, it became necessary to develop methods by which they could be integrated into civilized (white) society. Assimilation was forced upon the Native children in the form of boarding schools, where they were to be inculcated in civility, English, and Christianity. Attempts at assimilation would disinherit Indigenous peoples from thousands of years of traditions, essentially stripping them of their cultural identities. Traditional ways of living and being with the earth were denied them through enforcement of relocation programs, dispossessing them from the land and connections to their ancestors.

Manifest Destiny, those expansionist visions of America's frontier that continued the colonialization of America's first peoples and allowed for the decimation of entire tribes, is presented as progress in terms of American civilizational development and embraced in national remembrance as taming of the wild frontier and its savages. American legends and myths were created in this public space of knowing and memory creation, for the more a story is told, the more it becomes perceived and accepted as truth in public or national consciousness. A civilization built upon and held up by myths and legends is essentially constructed on lies—lies between the colonizers and the colonized, between State leaders and the people, lies of embellishment or omission—lies of Elite white fathers contrived for continuity of power for their white sons. The history of the American nation, the white colonizers' recreation of historical events has been presented as necessary for the establishment of a superior race and culture, for advancement of a civilized society as juxtaposed to primitive tribal life.

Construction of Indigenous peoples as savages was one method of dehumanizing them; to present them as less than men, more like animals, was to control public perception, thus, the Colonial Elites were tacitly approved and excused for the abuses, rapes, enslavement, removal, confinement, forced assimilation, and near annihilation of our First Peoples. Elite leaders in the modern era have time and again used differences from themselves to rationalize subjugation, oppression, and abuse of marginalized *others*, including women, Blacks, peoples of color, and LGBTQ. Patterns and continuities can be demonstrated throughout American history and are not subject to change. Unless, we, the people insist upon it—insist on equality, insist on justice, insist on liberty—for all peoples. We must reject the lies and half-truths, insisting on a deconstruction of official historical narratives and of the systems that have supported the deceit. Until we do, history will continue to repeat itself in oppressions of the many for the privilege of the few.

PART 2

Interlocking Systems of Privilege and Oppression

CHAPTER 7

Interlocking Systems of Privilege and Oppression

"Indeed, the interests of the oppressors lie in 'changing the consciousness of the oppressed, not the situation which oppresses them."

—Paulo Freire

American values espoused of individualism and self-sufficiency are constructed by the dominant members of society to keep all others in their respective places. Patriarchy as a social system, structured in domination and violence, intersects and interlocks with the economic system of Capitalism. Further, Democracy as America's political system, completes the triad of domination—the three systems being co-constituting, each attendant in reproduction of oppressions. Additionally, the United States government or State, as well as the individual states, have discretionary policing powers used to regulate behaviors and enforce order over matters related to the public's health and welfare.

Classification systems, inherent in patriarchy and capitalism, position individuals and groups of people for control. Constructed divisions based on gender, race and class allow for external and internal controls to be manipulated. Introduction of ideologies provides meaning and direction to the masses for expected and accepted ways of being and moving in the social world as constructed by the Elite.

Capitalism as the economic structure of the United States interlocks with Patriarchy and is operative in maintaining race differentials as well as, inequities based on gender, age, ability, and socioeconomic class. Capitalist, materialist consumerism is instilled in American consciousness via the media through consumer training and commercialism, promoting "socialization of desire". The appeal to consume, the desire for the next best thing, transcends socioeconomic class, however, the ability to respond is class dependent[25]. The Poor have no realistic expectation of having a piece of the pie, romantically referred to as the American Dream. Rather, the pursuit of the dream has become a waking nightmare for millions of Poor and working-class Americans struggling for day-to-day survival.

Additionally, capitalism as based in competition entreats each of us to get one-up on each other, and further, to have an expectation of ill-intent from the other party, as they, too, are attempting to elevate their position. Corporate interests are often contentious and set against concerns of laborers and environmental interest groups. Power dynamics allow for the Power Elite, members of the Transnational Capitalist Class (TCC)[26], to reign over a now global empire. Responsibility for degradation of the human condition and the environment is denied and/or projected back to the people who suffer. These same dynamics are used to position societal members as essentially in conflict with just about everyone; everyone who is not on our team or part of our social group or a member of our family. Indeed, rather than finding fault in the system that creates the tensions, we tend to blame each other and marginalized *others* for economic disparities, increases in violence, loss of jobs, etc. Rather than encouraging cooperation-based interaction and relationships, a capitalist mindset insists that someone (corporate personhood included) must win and with that, all others, by reasonable extension, must lose. And, winning may come at any cost as seen in the destruction of natural resources and tangential effects upon human and animal populations.

Democracy is a ruse used to offer members of American society a sense of belonging and a voice in political matters. As structural inequalities demonstrate, there is no real application of majority rule of, or power by the people, other than by inverted understanding, whereby there exists rule of the majority by the Elite few. Domination is based on the elevated position of a relatively few, as compared to the global population, corporatists, technocrats, and other elite men who dictate the economy, and social positioning and political actions of the masses from places far removed. Principles espoused by America's leaders of freedom, liberty, and justice for all, are most assuredly rhetorical as far too many members of society receive small measure of any.

Patriarchy, capitalism, and corporate elitist democracy are all structured for Elite white male domination and control of the masses. Together, these systems work in a complex web that intersects, interconnects, and interlocks all the elements of each to create conditions upon which a privileged Elite wield power over oppressed masses. The systems are entrenched and patterns and continuities in power can be demonstrated throughout American history. Divisions and strife between peoples work to the benefit of the Elite and keep the masses fragmented and isolated. Hierarchal classifications and constructed meanings attached to them allow for the *othering* of individuals and groups; a powerful tool the elite use to keep us separated and powerless. White supremacy, male dominance, elite-rule, and ethnocentrism are all grounded and embedded in our patriarchal, capitalist, faux democratic society, and we, each complicit in its continuation.

PATRIARCHY

CHAPTER 8

Patriarchy

"Patriarchy is like the elephant in the room that we don't talk about, but how could it not affect the planet radically when it's the superstructure of human society?"

— Ani DiFranco

The social system of most modern societies is patriarchy, the preemptive base upon, and social organization within, which networks of power intersect and interact. Patriarchy is the foundation upon which every individual in Western society is born and indoctrinated; since the family is the first institution where power dynamics are at play. A denial of this fundamental truth allows for convoluting of the multiple systems of oppression as developed within the social contexts of our white, heteropatriarchal, capitalist, predominantly Christian, and quasi-democratic society.

Patriarchy is broadly defined as control by men of a disproportionately large share of power. The establishment of a patriarchal system of control is the foundation of most of the world's Abrahamic religions, with the ultimate source of power as the Divine Father. There are elements found in religion which support all existing sociological theories, thus rather than distinguish one theory as above or opposed to the others; I submit that the theories overlap and intersect such that understanding can be garnered from each or all. My intention is not to deny the validity or importance of any religion to the people who ascribe to such, but purely for sociological reference.

The system of patriarchy is aided and abetted by the divine as a masculine entity as a tool for gender, race, and class oppression promoting stratification in its support of a hierarchy of people on earth, with the added injunction of subordination of humankind to Divine authority. Additionally, fundamentalist doctrines are interpreted and instructed such that only males of the faith can reach enlightenment or mastery. Religion has the power to shape collective beliefs, promoting a sense of belonging and collective consciousness, and thus, a cohesive social order. Further, it provides a cultural framework that supports the development of other social institutions through social cohesion. Social roles are constructed, defined, and refined through religion, norms identified and imposed, and attitudes and beliefs conforming to the group are enculturated.

Importantly, fundamental elements of religions inform gender roles and expectations not only for religious communities, but as prescriptions for moral code in larger society. Doctrines and conservative interpretations of text are used to advance subordination of females, not only supporting, but encouraging blame and shame. Additionally, legitimation of exclusion and even subjugation of *others* is interpreted as found in sacred texts. The same power dynamics which operate through religion, also inform, and instruct relationships in groups and of individuals through cultural inculcations.

Familial structure based in patriarchal and heteronormative terms dominant in American culture, identifies the male/father as head of household and the female/mother as subordinate, yet acting in congruence with the male. Children or progeny are subordinate to the male first, and then the female. The children then traditionally in line of succession of male born heirs are expected to receive their father's economic support and inheritance. Over time the familial structure has taken on new and ever-changing models; however, the normative, hetero-patriarchal model remains the dominant cultural scripting image. Thus, millions of single mothers raising their children are positioned outside of normative boundaries or deviant.

To call all males agents of women's oppression is to misunderstand the dynamics of power which operate within the structures of patriarchy, the politics of domination, and more significantly, that the control of society is wielded by an Elite few, not the whole of (man)kind or males, in general. Although these patterns, especially patterns of exclusion and domination, are manifested in personal arenas as well as the broader socio-political environment, these attitudes and behaviors have been acculturated over generations, and males are indoctrinated into the same systems in varying measures. Indeed, there are millions of superfluous males in this nation and globally who suffer multiple layers of oppression. Further, males especially in their formative years, often suffer psychologically and physically from psycho-social models of appropriate behaviors, dress, speech, etc., which hold them to standards of masculinity in much the same manner that females suffer as subordinate members of society, objectified, commodified, and identified against ideals of femininity.

Power dynamics between men and women are contentious as males and females are constantly positioning themselves relative to each other and others. In a patriarchal society, the politics of domination are inherently linked to hierarchal classifications based on social identifiers of gender, race, class, age, and ability. These differences are used to divide men from women, white from *other* races and ethnicities, rich from poor, educated from non-educated, old from young, and numerous other divisive classifications. Additionally, these contrived distinctions are instructive in the *other*ing of individuals and groups, creating animosity and inhibiting compassion.

White supremacist ideologies contribute to and are enabled by these distinctions. White supremacy is an interlocking system of patriarchy, racism, homophobia, ultra-nationalism, xenophobia, and religious fundamentalism, which creates and perpetuates a complex web of oppressions for women, the Poor, and peoples of color. The paradigm of whiteness and co-conspirators, heterosexuality, femininity, and masculinity have left huge psychic chasms for humanity; the chasms more readily identified as the "isms" created by stereotyping, labeling, and naming—dividing and separating people. The assumptions and contradictions inherent in these supposed frames of reference create and maintain divisions between people. These hierarchical patterns do much in maintenance of the status quo, undermining individual's self-actualization and allowing for continued systems of dominance and oppression.

These systems, then, are entrenched so deeply that social interaction is colored by sexism and racism at micro-levels in family-of-origin dynamics. Masculine and feminine roles and expectations of behavior are inculcated from birth. Normative models are further embedded through institutions of public education. Dominant ideologies of individualism and capitalism are indoctrinated through public education, as well as, duties of a good citizen/worker, a nationalist ethos, and the language of the dominant culture. Connections between ideologies, ethos, and expected behaviors are made within the walls of these institutions as each mind is enculturated into American society. In these spaces we develop understanding of who we are and where we fit in, if we fit in.

Within the system of patriarchy, we are all trying to figure out where we belong while society Elites decide for us. Sexism and racism are evident in patterns and continuities throughout history that are biased and exclusionary. Indeed, if we were to analyze historical data as applied in discriminatory practice, the only way to illustrate equitable distribution is from an inverted angle. From this vantage it becomes clear that women, especially Poor women, Indigenous peoples, and people of color are equally denied access to resources of housing, healthcare, education, and employment. These same groups of people are equally underrepresented in terms of justice; thus, disproportionate numbers are confined within the walls of our prison-industrial-complex. They have equal stakes in the devaluing of their persons through stereotyping, prejudices, and labeling. This is not how one would imagine equality of circumstance and access to resources to be applied; unless, one presupposes that one is a civilized, Elite, white man within a patriarchal society such as ours. Then equity becomes a "natural" circumstance of propertied, white males who may exercise their "natural" rights to subjugate colored *others* and women to preserve the privilege naturally attributed to them. The methods used to systematically discriminate against women and peoples of color may have changed, but equality remains a distant imagining for far too many.

The social system of patriarchy is based in and of Elite white male domination. Patriarchy in Western society and the United States of America, specifically, provides the foundational elements in white supremacy, genderism, and ethnocentrism supported further by paradigms of masculinity, heterosexuality, and femininity. Power dynamics and structural inequalities are created and maintained to keep individuals and groups within assigned parameters based on constructed differences based on race, ethnicity, sexuality, age, ability, and a myriad of other classifications. Further, ideologies have been purposefully institutionalized to provide rules, roles, beliefs, and attitudes for conformance to and support of Elite interests and adherence to the status quo.

CHAPTER 9

⚖

The Culture of Domination and Violence

"There are forms of oppression and domination which become invisible—the new normal."

— Michel Foucault

Historically, a culture of domination and violence has been created and maintained by Elite members of Western society to develop and enforce social controls. This culture infiltrates every crevice of being and living in American society. Government policing powers for the health and welfare of the public can be seen from the macrolevel to microlevel interactions as has been recently demonstrated in the government's response to civil unrest (ostensibly caused by government controls gone horribly awry). Further, federal, state, and local enforcement efforts in response to civil unrest are seen in increases in profiling, police brutality, and militarization.

Abuses of our nation's First Peoples, peoples of color, the poor, and immigrants by policing forces are patterned in power dynamics and have continued in varied forms throughout American history. Indeed, this system of domination is not particular to any point in modern time and can be found in some form throughout history in patterns and continuities. The issues functioned then as now, much as intended, to create perceptions of *threats* to security, to the status quo, to whatever it takes to make the masses of people compliant, submissive, dependent, powerless, and quite literally dispensable.

Socioeconomic structuring has led to an "underclass"[27] comprised of single mothers, young adults, peoples of color, elderly, and children; rendered "superfluous and non-functional"[28] in the development of global capitalism. Frustrated by lack of access to work, education, housing, and health care, and unable to meet basic needs, and further, unable to act against social and economic structures imposed upon them, the poor often turn to self-destructive measures as coping mechanisms. As functionless people they are likely to turn to alcohol and drugs, increasing domestic violence and delinquency. Further, crime functionally becomes a way to make ends meet[29]. In the criminalization of poverty, patriarchal society reacts to these markers of civil unrest using prejudicial statistics like youth bulges, citing increased criminal activity, delinquency, etc. to justify implementing measures for population control and punishment. The culture of domination supports these measures as racial profiling and police brutality increase as factors in the buildup of the prison-industrial complex. The explicit and implicit connections in power dynamics which create and maintain divisions based on gender, sexual orientation, race, class, ability, etc. are integral to how the establishment, adaptations, and buildup of the prison-industrial-complex has been appropriated as an instrument of control over the Poor of this nation[30].

The prisons have become the final measure of control of the Poor and other marginalized people and are "institutions for the criminal poor"[31], elements of society that are marked for exclusion at the most restrictive level. Our country has the largest incarceration rate of any country in the world, in large part due to the war on drugs; more effectively, a war on the poor. Incarceration as an instrument of social control, applies more broadly to all poor people, including millions of poor whites, increasingly, single mothers and their children.

The number of criminal offenses in this demographic has risen exponentially as laws are created for control and punishment of target population groups. The National Resource Center on Children and Families of the Incarcerated reports between the years of 1980 and 2011, the number of women in prison increased nearly 600% rising from just over 15,000 to nearly 112 thousand. Three years later, the numbers, including local jails, had risen to over 200,000 women; of those, over 120,000 are mothers of minor children[32]. Further, poor children, especially African American, Hispanic, poor whites, and Native American youth are often exposed to a loved one's incarceration, or they, themselves are targeted through school to prison pipelines and zero-tolerance policies.

> Paradoxically, our culture manipulates us to believe that anyone who breaks the law is a direct threat to us and our families, and that safety of all kinds, including economic security, can be guaranteed by watching, controlling, and caging the very people who suffer most from poverty, racism, and other forms of oppression[33].

The culture of domination which structures human interaction and behaviors is evident in macro and micro level dynamics. American society's acceptance of the politics of violence and domination can be observed both in repressive measures by State actors against marginalized groups and violence against females in public and private spheres. Thus, violence and domination are legitimized and normalized in Western society. Further, symbolic violence is evidenced in suppression of information, censorship, propaganda, and public relations; measures which are intended, and moreover work, to manipulate the masses to tacitly approve State decisions and actions. This public approval of State authority implies acceptance of invasions of privacy, controls of movement, and punitive measures for nonconformance in alleged exchange for public and personal security.

CHAPTER 10

Poverty As Violence Against Females and Multiple Oppressions of Others

"We have weapons of mass destruction we have to address here at home. Poverty is a weapon of mass destruction. Homelessness is a weapon of mass destruction. Unemployment is a weapon of mass destruction."

— Dennis Kucinich

Violence while normally associated with physical action against another, can be and is wielded in ideological manipulation and economic positioning. Even as the poor strive to meet American ideals of individual responsibility, their ranking as the lowest social class presents barriers to meeting those implied obligations. Many members of the poor, the lowest social class, are further degraded and classified as the "underclass"[34]. This class of people, single welfare mothers, peoples of color, indigenous, children, and superfluous males, are simultaneously excluded from participation in larger society yet, directed to be productive members of such. The chronic conditions of their existence in poverty create ever present stressors, hence, a traumatized mass of poor people exists in the richest and presumedly most advanced civilization in the world.

In "Of Witches, Welfare Queens, and the Disaster Named Poverty: The Search for a Counter-Narrative," author Shawn Cassiman introduces the idea of poverty as economic or structurally-caused violence by the state, through policy and propaganda against the population of poor, including their children. The result is trauma; experienced in levels of functioning, attachment, and health; thus, she suggests a trauma paradigm be considered, especially as discourse has become more focused on the pathological nature of dependency. Further, she links the trauma of poverty to disaster, in exposing poor members of society to a permanent state of alarm and anxiety[35].

The trauma of poverty is manifested in mental health problems of depression and anxiety. Further, trauma is embedded in the physical bodies of the Poor, thus embodiment of trauma presents as a glut of chronic illnesses. Single mothers and other members of the poor are at higher risk for post-traumatic stress disorder, generalized anxiety disorder, antisocial personality disorder, and substance abuse. As compared to the general population, the poor are more likely to have experienced childhood trauma in physical, sexual, or mental abuse. Living conditions for single mothers, their children, and millions of Poor offer little respite as they are likely to live in substandard housing and unsafe neighborhoods where the risk of violence is increased. Additionally, these mothers and their children are at high risk of being victims of domestic violence in some form. The trauma experienced results in decreased levels of functioning, attachment issues, and chronic health problems.

In "Research Regarding Low-Income Single Mothers' Mental and Physical Health: A Decade in Review," published in the Journal of Poverty, author C. Anne Broussard, PhD (2010) presents a discussion based on a 10-year review of literature related to health of low-income single mothers. She finds that low-income mothers continue to be vulnerable to multiple chronic risk factors which contribute to associated high risk for physical and mental health conditions. Physical health suffers from combinations of job insecurity, low-income work, lack of access to health insurance, and food insecurities. These conditions often are compounded by living in unsafe neighborhoods and poor quality housing where single mothers and their children have increased environmental risk, including violence. She finds that single mothers report more childhood trauma, in adversity and experience, more threats from life events, increased exposure to domestic violence, chronic deprivation, and stressors, as compared to members of the general population. Because of these factors, the author finds that low-income single mothers have higher likelihoods of suffering from posttraumatic stress disorder, generalized anxiety disorder, antisocial personality disorder, depression, substance abuse, and other disorders. Further, she suggests that impaired mental and emotional health for the mothers contributes to lowered ability to nurture and support their children and can contribute to use of more punitive disciplinary techniques. When focused on adolescent mothers and grandmothers in low-income groups, she finds that single, teen mothers suffer from multiple pregnancy-related conditions, including anemia, hypertension, toxemia, and eclampsia, as well as, mental health vulnerabilities to depression, low self-esteem, feelings of helplessness and hopelessness, and more attempted and completed suicides than older mothers. However, in turning the discussion to grandmothers who are raising or helping to raise grandchildren, and the associated health risks and conditions, the author finds in general, grandmothers suffer from the same emotional and physical stressors as single low-income mothers, and are prone to higher levels of depression and psychological distress than the general population. The author concludes that low-income, single mothers will continue to face multiple obstacles to self-sufficiency until policies and programs in the United States provide secure employment with living wages, and other support measures for children and their caretakers[36].

Women's public roles and behaviors have historically been instructed by and within social constructs. Hierarchal positioning inherent in patriarchy posits women as subordinate and submissive to men. Dichotomies in agency include male as actor and female as docile with females further dichotomized between virgin and slut. Politics of domination instruct these dynamics and are congruent with domestic violence and child abuse. Violence against women demonstrates the dynamics of power and domination as implicitly interacting with gender, sexuality, and agency. Interpersonal relationships are guided by cultural narratives, positioning men and women in an ongoing power struggle in the public and private spheres.

Domestic violence and abuse in all its forms demonstrate how the politics of domination inform culture at the microlevel. Social interaction at the interpersonal level is a direct reflection of the oppressive nature and violent control observed in macrolevel dynamics. Domestic violence follows a pattern referred to as a cycle of violence, which includes a tension-building stage, an explosive stage, and tranquil stage repeating over the course of the relationship. These same dynamics can be observed in the dynamic interplay between marginalized citizens and State agencies and actors; the state being the perpetrator of abuses and the citizens the victims. Dynamics between marginalized individuals and the State vary across space and time dependent on one's socio-politico-economic status and adaptation to or adoption of the status quo. The victims of abuse, the Poor, moreover, take the abuses of their civil rights as natural to their allotted station.

Forming opposition to violence against females, as well as, oppression of any person or group of people, rests on an understanding of the social system of patriarchy, the inherent politics of power, and the culture of domination and violence which inform and support it, and, by extension, direct the everyday lives of all citizens, here and abroad. Tools of control wielded by Power Elites position the American public as a mind manipulated mass that is fully onboard with national and international policy impositions which have wreaked havoc all over the globe in increased poverties and degradation of the planet. Americans, male and female, black and white, young, and old are imagined to be either complacent or complicit participants in imposition of a capitalist world order by intimidation and force.

CAPITALISM

CHAPTER 11

Capitalism

"It turned out that capitalism alone could make people not only rich and happy but also poor, hungry, miserable, and powerless."

—Masha Gessen

The economic structure of the United States operates to maintain gender, race, and class differentials for manipulation of power dynamics in socioeconomic positioning of individuals and whole groups of people. Economic trends affecting poverty, the internationalization of capital, a direct result of multinational corporations, and transformation of the world's division of labor have effectively pulled out the middle rungs of the economic ladder, thus positioning the working middle class against the poor, and pitting poor against poor. Further, the technological revolution with the introduction of robotized, automated production has made human production dispensable, which has led to technological unemployment. This has created a shift in the distribution of income and wealth, polarizing society into the handful of ultra-rich and an ever-expanding mass of Poor. By giving control of the nation's means of production to private and multinational corporations, funding industrial growth, and limiting labor's ability to mount an offensive, the United States government essentially paved the way for the corporate state. The bottom line or profit-driven economics have informed politics such that consideration of the people and the environment is limited, if at all.

Legitimization of economic structuring, whereby Capitalism and its tenets become ingrained in consciousness enables and institutionalizes genderism, racism, classism, and ableism as people at the bottom of the economic ladder are deemed dispensable. Women, especially, single heads-of-households and their children, and people of color occupy this bottom rung leading to discourse surrounding the feminization of poverty. The "feminization of poverty"[37] and the feminization of migration have become patterns of human development with root causes in economic and social systems structured in male-dominated terms.

Class consciousness, as well as gender and race consciousness, have been continually diverted by entertainment, consumerism, and fear-based tactics, replaced by conflict and divisions of a more suitable nature, or made to appear antiestablishment, socialist influenced, and unpatriotic. Thus, although the disparities between the Elite and just about everybody else have continued to increase in economic and political measures, speaking of such things, especially as a citizen of America, the pillar of freedom and justice, implies a displaced hypercriticality and radical left-wing leanings, etc. Internal agitators to the status quo are thus labeled and essentially usurped of their influence.

In a capitalist economic structure, the accumulation of wealth denotes elevated socioeconomic status, that status conveys privilege, and with that privilege, comes power. This power is intrinsically connected to an ethics of domination, which implies that those in power have a right to rule over the powerless and use whatever means necessary to make and keep them subordinate. Power over equates to oppression of, and the oppressions are multiple, intersectional, entrenched, and now, global. If to bleed white is by definition; to deprive of all resources, then globalization has in effect, bled the world white.

Globalization is the process by which the Global Elite have introduced and entrenched their interests and aspirations worldwide as seen in neoliberalism and neocolonialism. Under the guise of development, corporatists and technocrats have manipulated foreign governments into selling off their countries' natural and man-made [labor] resources. The very measures by which inequality was to be leveled, in fact, have contributed to socio-economic patterns referred to as the feminization and criminalization of poverty and the feminization of migration. These patterns reflect how power relations structured by and within our social and economic systems allow for the Elite to construct people's lives patterned by and arranged relative to race, gender class, religion, ability, and other classifications.

The dynamic interplay of economic restructuring and government controls evident locally has far-reaching implications in the global community. Indebted foreign nations surrender to conditionalities, imposed by the International Monetary Fund (IMF), implementing structural adjustment policies, and surrendering national resources, natural and man-made [labor]. People have no choice in consumption of water, healthcare, and food, making these prime targets for privatization. However, due to privatization and international consumption rates, the Indigenous peoples are robbed of these resources as water, blue gold, is sold to the highest foreign bidder and other natural resources are similarly disposed. The human element is simultaneously disregarded and commodified. Labor flexibility is written into World Bank loans for ease in manipulation of working conditions and wages to maximize profit. Workers who find employment face abhorrible conditions, while thousands of others must migrate in search of work and survival. Immigration is an integral part of the dynamism of US capitalism, controlling the ebb and flow of an available (global) labor force. When peasant farmers and Indigenous peoples protest these conditions, they are labeled insurgents and terrorists. The US government begins a media campaign to raise fundamentalist social consciousness to create a national syndrome, thereby rationalizing provisions for implementing imperialist military control of these populations.

Socioeconomic positioning of masses of Poor in America and globally demand a critical evaluation of the system of capitalism. The Power Elite have implemented free market economics all around the world. The doctrine of laissez-faire not only allows the market and corporate leaders freedom to do what they may, it is an injunction to State leaders to keep their hands off and governments out, unless, of course, it is in support of Elite capitalist agendas. The system of capitalism creates inequalities—in income, in status, in power, in resources, in quality of life. Without deconstruction of the system and introduction of regulations on corporate masters, disparities in wealth and circumstance will grow exponentially.

CHAPTER 12

Buying In: Consumerism, Conformance, Commodification, and Consumption

"The essence of capitalism is to turn nature into commodities and commodities into capital. The live green earth is transformed into dead gold bricks, with luxury items for the few and toxic slag heaps for the many. The glittering mansion overlooks a vast sprawl of shanty towns, wherein a desperate, demoralized humanity is kept in line with drugs, television, and armed force."

—Michael Parenti

As consumers in a patriarchal, capitalist society we are expected to conform to ideologies that support the market and contribute to growth. There is no written contract for expected behaviors and beliefs, rather it is an implied understanding, inherent in a system we are born and indoctrinated into. The ideologies of the system, the institutionalized beliefs, are parts of the invisible authority of the social, economic, and political systems of human control. We conform in appearance, attitudes, and actions; thus, we legitimize the messages and perpetuate the systems. Additionally, messages of consumption, of what, why, and how much to consume are inescapable as mass media fills our eyes and ears with images and messages.

Consumerism founded in basic needs, has been replaced by a system of consumption and waste that leaves people fragmented, isolated, and desperate. Basic needs are replaced with market-driven ideas of needs filled by things we can consume. With the next best thing out there, the message repeats; anyone can buy health, happiness, beauty, and material desires. This consumerist mindset is what the capitalist system builds corporate empires on; thus, in a very real sense, our collective needs feed corporate greed and then, corporate greed feeds us, our needs. The capitalist imperative for growth at all costs, quite literally posits profit over people. Evidence of this is in the profit-laden beauty and health industries commodification of the human body and products for maintenance and improvement. Further, the consumerist mentality is molded by mass media toward conformance to feminine ideals, achievable through consumption of goods sold.

Beauty is in the eye of the beholder; so, the saying goes. But, as beholders within the systems of patriarchy and capitalism our standards of beauty are dictated by the politics of appearance. These politics are orchestrated by the male-dominated beauty and health industries using media-driven popular culture in structuring our attitudes, beliefs, and actions toward beauty. Further, the male gaze inscribes the female body with meaning, definitions of femininity, including ideals of beauty, preferred female behaviors in cultural roles, and value in a capitalist society. As Sheila Jeffreys suggests in "Making Up Is Hard to Do," "what is beautiful is constructed politically and incorporates race, class, and sex prejudices.[38]" The idealized female body as an object directed by and for the male gaze becomes a commodity.

The beauty and health industries have seized on this commodification in a big way, reinscribing the feminine ideal as attainable with the purchase of their products. And, in our consumer-driven society, beauty and thinness become goals by which females determine and increase their value. This becomes apparent when considering the billions of dollars spent annually by girls and women on beauty products, plastic surgery, and diet aids. And, as Jeffreys notes, "cosmetic manufacturers make profits from selling both the cause of the problem and solutions for it."[39]

The beauty ideal is so profit-laden, it has been directed in recent decades toward males, as well. As Susan Bordo suggests in "Beauty, (Re)Discovers the Male Body", "more and more men are landing straight into the formerly female territory of body-image dysfunction, eating disorders, and exercise compulsion."[40] The media, beauty industry and health industry are so effective in promoting the feminine and masculine ideals that thousands of girls and women and now men, too, are killing themselves to reach it. Herein is offered explanation of how the objectification and commodification of the female body, subscribed to by our culture and society, and projected by the beauty industry, promoted by the mainstream media, and perpetuated by the health industry has created a crisis in women's health.

The beauty/fashion, media, and health industries work in conjunction to create the feminine ideal of beauty and then, simultaneously making girls and women feel inadequate, while also offering them ways to look and thus, feel better. The images of the ideal are everywhere in popular culture and that ideal is young, thin, and white. In her article "The More You Subtract, the More You Add", Jean Kilbourne addresses the obsession with thinness in our society and writes, "The big success story of our entertainment industry is our ability to export insecurity. We can make any woman anywhere feel perfectly rotten about her shape."[41] The appeal to conform to the ideal operates across race, age, and class lines, and as the author states, it is a ". . . message apparent in popular culture, the message that she should diminish herself, she should be less than she is."[42] In collusion with this message is the ever-evident appreciation of a youthful appearance, prompting the increasing trends toward surgical and chemical modifications. Further, the more insidious message is, if you are flawed, you can be fixed.

In "Feminist Theory, the Body, and the Disabled Figure", Rosemarie Garland-Thomson discusses the "parallels between the social meanings attributed to female bodies and those assigned to disabled bodies.[43]"

Indeed,

> ...the language of contemporary cosmetic surgery presented in women's magazines persistently casts the unreconstructed female body as having 'abnormalities' that can be 'corrected' by surgical procedures which 'improve' one's appearance... these changes are imagined to be choices that will sculpt the female body, so it conforms to a feminine ideal[44].

Desire has turned into obsession. Women's quest for beauty has built profit empires for the media, health, beauty, and fashion industries. But, even as the costs to their health mount, commodification and commercialization of the female body continues.

The pressures to conform to the beauty ideal result in females subjecting their bodies to strict diet regimens, untested pharmaceuticals for weight loss, toxins in beauty products used on skin, face, and hair, and dangers from surgical and chemical alterations. In addition to physiological health issues, women's mental health is being profoundly adversely affected. The connection between the media saturation surrounding beauty and the effects on females' mind/body well-being is that, as Kilbourne states, "Mass communication has made possible a new kind of national peer pressure that erodes private and individual values and standards."[45] The values of larger society are adopted or enculturated and internalized to such a degree as to become a preoccupation, thus females' mental health is compromised in perpetual attempts at conformance.

This preoccupation manifests in eating disorders like anorexia and bulimia, in plastic surgery mania, depression, and most alarmingly, in suicide. As Kilbourne states, "Girls are made to feel so terrible about themselves that they would rather be dead, than fat."[46] These medical conditions are "in a sense standard feminine script writ large enough to become disabling conditions, blurring the line between normal female behavior and pathology."[47] Normative behaviors for feminine hygiene and appearance dictate use of body hair removal products, hair dyes and perms, and makeup. And, although "feminization alterations increase a woman's cultural capital,"[48] they simultaneously render the female body disabled. The disabled female body is then made well or whole again, through use of additional health and beauty products and procedures.

In true patriarchal, capitalist style, society answers these mental and physical health issues in what Marcy Jane Knopf-Newman argues is "dominant rhetoric that blames women's lifestyle choices rather than investigating larger system cause of the disease . . ."[49] Knopf-Newman addresses the causes of breast cancer in "Public Eyes", where she illustrates the need to "look for answers in larger social, political, and institutional forces."[50] The feminine ideal created by the male-gaze and reaffirmed by popular culture, has in turn, created a feminine dilemma. The Reproductive Justice Agenda captures how the personal is political and conversely, the political is personal in creating this dilemma; "women's bodies, reproduction and sexuality are often used as the excuse and the target for unequal treatment in the attempt to control our communities [minority communities]."[51]

The female body has been manipulated as a status symbol, a sexual fantasy, and a profit-marker. In disregard, society offers paltry compensation while girls and women get pulled under the wheels of hegemony. The old adages "no pain, no gain" and "beauty is pain" are renewed, reavowed, and reified in disturbing fashion. In "The Body Politic", Abra Fortune Chernik writes of her struggle with anorexia; explaining that in starving herself, she was able to exercise some form of control in her life. But, she expounds, "I starved away my power, and vision, my energy and inclinations."[52] In adopting the feminine ideal of beauty as formulated and prescribed in popular culture women, are in effect, giving up their power to self-actualization. The politics of appearance are deeply entrenched in our society. The costs of continuing to subscribe to male notions of beauty must be challenged for the sake of women's health.

The female body has been inscribed with meaning. Meaning defined by patriarchy and capitalism. Women must claim authority to demand femininity be defined in their terms. Chernik explains the compelling reasons for her eventual healing from anorexia after years of suffering in a vain attempt to fit into the feminine beauty ideal, stating, "I had been willing to accept self-sabotage, but now I refused to sacrifice myself to a society that profited from my pain."[53] A profit-making, male-dominated empire continues to drive the ideal into consciousness, individual and collective.

But, in awakening to their true feminine potential, women must, as suggested by Asian Communities for Reproductive Justice, continue to challenge patriarchal social relations and addressing the intersection[s] of racism, sexism, and class oppression. Perhaps then, "we will be able to build the collective social, economic, and political power of all women and girls to make choices that protect and contribute to our reproductive health and overall well-being."[54]

We, females, and males, are bombarded with messages of how best to fit constructed, gendered roles in conformance to cultural compulsions and expectations. Appearance is dictated to such a profound degree that many people construct their identities around illusory ideals. The media, health, and beauty industries have conspired in institutionalizing the ideals in public consciousness, and we have each bought into the messages in consumption, material and ideological. In the process, as Bordo suggests, "we substitute individualized beauty—the distinctive faces" of generations of races and cultures "for generic, very often racialized, reproducible codes of youth."[55]

Capitalism requires consumer commitment to conformance and consumption. In compliance, we have adapted to modern society adopting a mechanized routine of interaction for people with other people, with things, and with the environment. This routine is based in a marketplace culture where people are enculturated in Americanism (Westernization) with values of individualism and capital/cultural accumulation. Further, commodification of nearly everything tangible has created a society in which value is placed in material objects and by which the human body has been introduced to the market for profit. Desire is created by corporate-driven media messages surrounding the latest trends, as needs and wants are confused in consumer consciousness.

CHAPTER 13

The Global Power Elite and The Crises of Capitalism

"Capitalism will behave antisocially if it is profitable for it to do so, and that can now mean human devastation on an unimaginable scale. What used to be apocalyptic fantasy is today no more than sober realism."

—Terry Eagleton

In posing sociological inquiries of Who Wins, Who Loses, and Who Decides, dynamics of power are illuminated for closer inspection. So too, are numerous structural inequalities created by the Elite to maintain power and to keep all *others* in their respective places. Throughout this text references are made to American capitalists and the Power Elite/Global Power Elite. In *Giants: The Global Power Elite*, author Peter Phillips introduces us to them; "Gulfstream/private jet-flying, megacorporation-interlocked, policy-building Elites of the world—people at the absolute peak of the global power pyramid."[56] Yes, they are real! And, provided in his compilation are the names and affiliations of the Global Elite! Though they make up less than thirty percent of the global population, they own and control almost all the world's assets and resources; a small percentage of which, <5% is left for the rest of us. And, they want that, too!

Historically, the dominant power players in America have been white, propertied, and heterosexual men; this dynamic has changed little, as even today "70% are male, eighty-four percent are white"[57] and mostly from North America and Europe. They are the Transnational Capitalist Class (TCC), and they rule the world—all of it! They are all interconnected, either personally, professionally, or politically. The ideologies they subscribe to are the same ones which they use to manipulate the rest of the world's population, capitalism and its central doctrine, individualism as demonstrated through self-reliance.

> Transnational [Capitalist Class] Power Elites hold a common ideological identity of being the engineers of global capitalism, with a firm belief that their way of life and continuing capital growth is best for all humankind[58].

Their individual egos and collective identity beliefs are not in keeping with the betterment of humankind nor the ecological preservation of the planet. Perhaps, as individuals, Elite members of society have some measure of compassion and empathy. However, the group ego, the mindset, gives every indication of being a narcissist. This idea is conceivable considering corporations have been given legal status as persons and corporate leaders influence the dynamic interplay between States and citizen members. The Elite have historically manipulated scientific understandings to pathologize dependency; thus, this is simply an inverted application. If indeed, as Peter Phillips of *Giants* suggests, their "social consciousness carries over into daily life . . . giving them a continuing sense of importance and prestige,"[59] then the following assessment fits. He, the narcissist, herein understood to be members of the TCC, believes himself to be important and seeks this validation from others, he lacks empathy, is arrogant, and believes he is entitled to everything he wants. So, then, his focused self-importance and complete disregard for everyone else is pathological. He will always win, others will always lose, and he will always decide. The pathological narcissist, in his sickness, will tear down everyone around him and blame them for their misery. The parallels in the foregoing analogy are striking, if not disturbing.

> The most important concern for the Transnational Capitalist Class (TCC) is protecting capital investment, ensuring debt collection, and building opportunities for further returns. If protecting the environment is profitable, then green investments are acceptable. What remains unacceptable is the spending of money on people . . . and services [for the people] that do not benefit capitalism[60].

Indeed, this focus on capital returns at any cost is recognizably at extreme cost in terms of human health and well-being, thus, we are experiencing "a crisis in capitalism."[61] For millions of Americans and hundreds of millions globally, this crisis is lived in day-to-day struggles for sustenance and survival.

According to Michael Harrington, author of *The New American Poverty*, "There is a new poverty which is systemic and the result of massive economic and social transformations and is more intersectional and tenacious than ever before in history."[62] The economic trends contributing to ever-increasing global poverties are:

1) The internationalization of capital, a direct result of the spread of multinationals, corporations with loyalty to no nation, which are led by the Global Power Elite and facilitated by the World Trade Organization (WTO), has led to the devastation of human lives and the environment.[63]

2) Transformation of the world's division of labor has contributed to an occupational restructuring whereby the middle rungs of the economic ladder of mobility have been pulled out, essentially positioning the middle working class against the working poor, and pitting poor against poor. Massive worldwide unemployment uproots workers in every advanced country; the workers are, in turn, rooted to institutional economic racism.[64]

3) The technological revolution which introduced robotized, automated production, has made human production dispensable, which has led to "technological unemployment," creating a basic shift in the distribution of income and wealth.[65]

The crises of capitalism can be described as a lack of care and displacement of value. The Power Elite who control the world's resources, care little if at all, as is evidenced by the masses of people in poverty, depletion of natural resources, and the exploitation of the earth. Value is not found in the people nor the planet apart from how they might contribute as profit models.

As natural disasters increase in occurrence and severity, ice shelves drop into the ocean, and the massive desertification of once arable lands continue, global warming is conveniently denied, or blame projected onto the people. COVID lockdowns of the global population were made sufferable, not in contribution to saving human lives, but moreover, as proof that we, the people, caused the pollution and our absence from public life fixed it. And, while we each are responsible for waste and pollution, our contribution is negligible in comparison to the debasement of the earth by corporations. The entire blame cannot reasonably be laid at the people's feet, rather it must be mitigated in cause and consequence by the Elite in control of transnational corporate abuses of the earth.

CHAPTER 14

⚖

The Shock Doctrine: America's Induction Into The Global Capitalist Order

"Global capitalism is simply accepted as a fact that you cannot do anything about. The only question is, Will you accommodate yourself to it, or will you be dismissed and excluded?"

— Slavoj Žižek

The terms by which deregulated Capitalism operate have been institutionalized within our language system as modifiers. In a curious play on words, we can describe as *free*, the very economic system which has led to the global shackling of billions of people in bonds of poverty. This is not a coincidence, according to Naomi Klein, author of *The Shock Doctrine: The Rise of Disaster Capitalism*, rather, it demonstrates that the rhetoric of freedom has often been employed as part and parcel of global capitalism. Milton Friedman, noted economist and thought leader within the Chicago School of Economics, played on these associations, introducing the *free* market system as a perfect scientific system. "Based on the premise that if every individual acted in their own self-interest (freely chosen, of course), the system would create the maximum benefits for all."[66] The system works according to Friedman, if it is unencumbered by restraints, i.e., *free*. For the system to be free to function optimally, however, governments must follow rules of the market, imposing economic reforms Klein refers to as the "free-market trinity":[67] privatization, deregulation, and cuts to social spending. These rules do little to confine the movements of the Elite, but effectively deprive the general population of public resources and allow for corporations to deny responsibility for industrial damages while simultaneously deflecting problems as created by the people.

Klein challenges the notion that deregulated capitalism, the new economic world order was "born of freedom, that unfettered free-markets go hand-in-hand with democracy."[68] The challenge is presented in an introduction to what she refers to as the "Shock Doctrine", the method by which US corporate and political Elites, with the support of government-sponsored media propaganda and military force, have imposed a capitalist world order. The "Shock Doctrine" is implemented in three steps:

> First, the initial shock from a "crisis" of a war, economic or social breakdown, or natural disaster; followed by shock therapy in the form of massive economic reforms; and, finally, shock therapy in the form of political terror, physical imprisonment, and torture, and sometimes death for any "resistors to the imposed system."[69]

The violent imposition of the free-market system has been applied by the *Shock Doctrine* to Third World developmentalism and nationalism. Violence and repressive measures, rather than freedom and democracy, have accompanied the economic founding of a new economic world order. She states, "corporatist alliance is in the midst of conquering its final frontier: closed oil economies of the Arab world, and sectors of Western economies (American)."[70] This statement should be a flashing red light to anyone who is paying attention. The work of exploring linked operations of the economic, political, and social spheres in the process of world transformation popularly referred to as globalization is crucial, if not critical, and Klein's is a brave stance and one that must be taken.

America's people were introduced to their own "Shock Doctrine" on September 11, 2001 with the bombing of the Twin Towers, the Pentagon, and the downing of Flight 93. The strike was on the heart of capitalism and the American state as the blood that keeps it beating. Americans, rather than making this connection, internalize the government's propaganda, the "official" truths that foster then nurture mythology. The official story is presented thusly, American citizens, on this date, became the victims and post-traumatic stress survivors of Islam-fascist attacks due to a breech in our national security that enabled *terrorists* to launch an offensive on American soil. The mainstream media's depiction of events, before, during, and after led the American people to believe that *terrorists* were responsible for the attack on our nation and that our moral imperative was to put an end to *evil* by responding with an all-out, no-holds-barred, "War on Terror." The axis of evil had essentially brought America and its people its national emergency, its crisis, an external threat, and one that could and did infiltrate national security. The fact that it occurred in our homeland left Americans understandably awestruck, shocked, terrified, grieving. While citizens were reeling from our national shock, our perilous leaders stepped up as our stalwart defenders mobilizing troops, and in defense of our freedoms decided it was in our collective best interest to institute "Homeland Security" measures. So, with the public's consent (well, sort of), in our collective distorted sense of reality, as the shock of the bombings left us frightened and confused, an acquiescent opening of a sort allowed for the buildup of a national security and surveillance system though legally implemented via The USA Patriot Act.

But, even after the dust settled, the debris was removed (post-haste), the dead were mourned (as they are still), the devils in disguise unmasked, and a whole country targeted for invasion and ultimately, destruction; there were lingering laments and doubts. The loss of so many lives was cause enough for immense, national sorrow; but, the twisted timelines, less-than rapid response, questionable official accounts, and lack of transparency and accountability surrounding the attacks, left a gaping wound in the hearts of many Americans—resulting in a resounding call from the American public for Truth. Our government's use of its citizens' pain was subterfuge working to the decided advantage of what Klein refers to as the "disaster capitalism complex."[71] That is, disasters are profitable for the owners of capital. Questions were answered with lies or deflections aimed at the evildoers, leaving many patriots skeptical, and leading those to conspire in an effort to know, what really happened on that fateful day in September[?].

To raise awareness surrounding the events, before, during and after 9/11, intellectuals from numerous disciplines looked for and found answers to unanswered questions, and then expounded on those for the world audience in a compilation of essays published in *9/11 and American Empire: Intellectuals Speak Out*. Perhaps, as Richard Falk states in "Global Ambitions and Geopolitical War: The Domestic Challenge"*:*

> Momentous suspicious events bearing on the legitimacy of the process of governance in the United States have been consistently shielded from mainstream inquiry by being inscribed as the wild fantasies of *conspiracy theorists*.[72]

Still, it is our civic duty, a moral obligation, and right guaranteed us as citizens of the United States of America, to "petition the Government for a redress of grievances."[73] So, it is then, that herewith, I join the *conspiracy theorists*; not in "wild fantasy," but in critical discernment of heinous acts perpetrated by our Government against all of humanity, as well as, a rational consideration of the instruments, tools, measures, etc. used to manipulate and control the American people as accomplices, however unknowing, in a Global Domination Project.

The atrocities of war crimes committed in defense of freedom for the people of this nation in perpetual "War(s) on Terror" are indefensible. Yet, the military apparatus of the global capitalist machine continues; even as America's debt spirals out of control, billions of dollars are appropriated for defense funding. As words like genocide, torture, disappearances, gang-rape, expropriation of natural resources, and the killing of millions of civilians in Iraq, appear to be routine forms of expression that slip through our mass consciousness without qualm or question, one must surely ponder: How does this happen? When did we become so callous and indifferent? Do the people of America know what is happening around the globe for the sake of their freedoms? Do they care? Are they simple pawns in a capitalist power game played out on a global stage? These are important questions and deserve the utmost care in consideration as we are being judged, individually and collectively, by the globalized world's people. By accepting official government statements as truth, we as Americans allow ourselves to be duped by the system. In the long run, neither embarrassment nor shame will excuse our blind acceptance, whether due to mass ignorance or mere complacency.

The War on Terror and his domestic ally, Homeland Security, operate on the "unending mandate of protecting the US homeland in perpetuity while eliminating all 'evil' abroad."[74] The corporatist agenda remains hidden even as increased surveillance, mass incarceration, and civil liberties are trampled on, here in the land of the free. This also, rather conveniently, allows for continued and ever-increasing expenditures for military/defense/security spending and a corresponding transfer of private debts to public hands as social programs are cut to fund the Power Elite's agenda. If the War on Terror has truly become a "war against all obstacles to the new order"[75] as argued by Klein, then it follows that the people of America are both the final obstacle and the last defense. Everything is in place for the next big threat, crisis, disaster—be it economic, natural, or cultural, to be used as the springboard for the final phase of operation "Shock America."

The powers available to any President of the United States of America, as Commander-in-Chief include: the power to declare a "national state of emergency" by which the National Guard may be used to impose and enforce martial law on the citizens of this country; the use of invasive surveillance systems or the ability to halt internet communications access altogether; to arrest and incarcerate masses of people, and just basically trample on civil rights—all while operating under the legal confines of our Constitution and in the broader interests of the people. President Trump has already used some of these tools in response to threat of invasion by an unseen enemy but one far-reaching in lethal effects, the global pandemic of COVID-19. Some tools have been used against immigrants and their children within our country's borders as seen in the overcrowded, unsanitary, unsafe, and inhumane camps filled with immigrant children separated and held from their parents. Additionally, the tools have been used to suppress recent demonstrations against police brutality towards black people. Even when there has been peaceful protest by demonstrators, there has been increasing use of a weaponized police force to quell any potential unrest. This is harrowing stuff! The messages in *The Shock Doctrine* should scare us; they should slap us in the face and scream, "WAKE UP!" They might even make us sad and piss us off, too. These emotions are scarce what we will surely feel as America joins the rest of the global economic order and its citizens suffer the same as people of other shocked nations.

Unfettered capitalism has created a torrent of ill effects in social, economic, and ecologic conditions. The marriage of global capitalist aspirations to America's imperialist ambitions has allowed for the creation of a Transnational Capitalist Class (TCC), an elite group who have all but cornered the market all around the world. They decide who wins and who loses; and, the odds are ever in their favor. The separation between them and you or me, or the rest of the world's people for that matter, is expansive, and the space between void of care. If care is to be found in the space between our Elite leaders and ourselves, it is care for unfettered capital growth and we, the American people, are an encroachment.

CHAPTER 15

The Global Domination Project: Empire Building and Perma-War

"For most of the history of the American empire, government has been a tool for preserving and furthering the power and might of white male corporate elites."

—Cornel West

The American public/collective consciousness has historically been manipulated in such a manner that popular support appears to lend itself to economic, social, and political policies of the United States government, both domestic and foreign. This statement is evidenced in the conventional presentation and acceptance of America in the role of the "great crusade[r]"[76] of the Second World War against the great enemies of Nazi fascism and Japanese militarism on a "divine mission to save the world."[77] Further, this historical rendering maintains that American policies were thus guided by ideals of justice, freedom, and democracy. This interpretation of America's role demonstrates the mythologizing of history; that is, history manipulated to serve specific goals or ends, or what might also be referred to as state-sought reality making. There is energy and even power in a great myth as illuminated in *The Myth of the Good War: America in the Second World War,* by author Jacques R. Pauwels. He argues, then demonstrates, the myth as created and maintained by government and media propaganda directly influenced by industry, military, and other American Elites. Acceptance by the public and perpetuation of the myth in mass consciousness allows for "continuity and consistency of Washington policy . . . guided by the interests of American industry;"[78] most significantly, industry benefiting in, of, and by way(s) of war-making.

Pauwels applies a collective paradigm based on the ideas of Chomsky, Williams, Kolko, Parenti, and C.W. Mills. The synthesized paradigm argues that:

> The development of the capitalist economy requires that the American social, economic, and therefore, also political Elites consistently pursue their class interests, at home and abroad . . . without much regard for the values of democracy, liberty, and justice of which America claims to be the great champion. [79]

The paradigm applied to historical analyses, challenges conventional wisdom by asking difficult questions such as, "Who profited? Qui Bono?" and "Why did the United States **really** go to war?"[80] Answers are provided by introduction of "dirty truths" which are intended to provoke reflection upon the myth as based on the "comfortable official truth." This reflection allows for a break from the myth and further, consideration of the relevance of inconvenient truths in American historical development, as well as, present and future policy developments and the relative implications for the American people and the world-at-large. That is, a critical evaluation of America's role before, during, and after WWII, is as the author notes, " . . . not only a right but also a duty."[81] By accepting official government statements as "truth," we, as Americans, allow ourselves to be duped by the system. In the long run, neither embarrassment nor shame will excuse our blind acceptance, whether due to mass ignorance or mere complacency. The myth of the "good war"[82] has allowed for America's Power Elite to continue with business as usual at the expense of nearly everyone else in the world. Through the control of information and manipulation of its meaning, America's leaders have time and again, molded a pliant mass public consciousness to meet their ends and continue to do so even now. Meanwhile, the United States government, at the direction of business, industry, military, and media leaders, has behaved badly for the sake of a capitalist world order and, at the expense of the world's general population, not excluding American citizens.

Facts introduced in opposition to the long-held myth carry a great deal of weight in countering any good that was to come of US intervention in World War II. There are numerous valid and important counter truths—from lucrative corporate involvement with Nazi Germany, to the United States government's post-war support of the same European Elites who knowingly compromised their respective countries and their people to fascism pre-war. As disturbing as these counter truths are, moreover, their exposure serves to illuminate just how powerful the myth is in contributing to the "collective brainwashing"[83] of the American people. By introducing the myth of the "good war," as well as the many smaller myths within, and further, in providing a frighteningly convincing counterview, Pauwels illustrates how Elitist agendas follow a defined trajectory, one which leads inevitably to a unilateral, militarized, capitalist world order. The word democratic is omitted from this description as the notion of democracy has little to do with the path of American Elites and their global counterparts.

World War II presented as "a window of opportunity"[84] for American business and industry leaders, the Elites; the path to power leading from

American corporate Elite headquarters to the Oval Office of the White House. Further, as evidenced in US economic, social, and political policies, enacted by laws, implemented by military and policing efforts, and allegedly supported in accordance with the mythology, by a unified nationalistic American public. The path was not, as we have been led to believe, one of moral righteousness or worldly beneficence, but was in fact, a path of deceit, paved by innuendo and propaganda and marked in blood and carnage; all for the sake of almighty capital. The government of the United States in providing the keys to control of the nation's means of production to private corporations and further, in funding industrial growth and limiting labor's ability to mount an offensive, essentially paved the way for the corporate state.

While American citizens have explored the limits of their freedoms, citizens of the new international world order are subject to the whims of big business much as they were half a century ago. Though the United States has amassed an empire on the backs of the global poor, the truth of our country's imperial ambitions has been "masked in the rhetoric of freedom."[85] The American government has continually acted with utter disregard for the wants and desires of the global population. Rather, in acting as "leader of the free world" and establishing a new international economic order, we have exacted the American worldview by shows of military might and use of such devices as "considerations" written into the Lend-Lease arrangements and adoption of "Open-Door" principles at the United Nations Monetary and Financial Conference in Bretton Woods. Further, in the use of post-war instruments such as "conditionalities" imposed on the governments of nations indebted to the International Monetary Fund (IMF) and the World Bank, American multi-nationals and transnational corporations have continued to maintain economic control. When the common people of these nations have sought rectification for having been stripped of their natural resources and their self-determination, they are labeled as agitators, resistors, rebels, insurgents, and terrorists.

These readily applied labels have become watchwords in twenty-first century politics, but the dynamics behind them were first to be acted on during the era referred to as the "Cold War." Communism post-World War II presented both an ideological and an economic counter-model to

"Democratic-Capitalism;" one the American government and its Elite corporate sponsors could ill afford. Thus, the demonization of the Soviet people was a necessary part of the Cold War, which was waged in propaganda and innuendo launched by the mainstream media and government entities. Ideological differences between the United States and Russia proved to be the focal points of contention. However, as history would have it, these differences were exaggerated and often misrepresented by the media; such that Americans would not only be intimidated by this media-hyped external threat, but be hyper-vigilant against communist infiltrators, "Reds," in their midst. The paranoia was whipped into such a frenzy that McCarthyism swept the nation, and the people of America saw friends and neighbors put on trial to defend their reputations and national allegiance. The express purpose of this propaganda was to disturb the American people's sense of security to such a degree that they would readily support a general build-up in nuclear-powered arms and other military expenditures—and it worked.

The Second World War posited the United States of America as a world superpower, economically, militarily, and politically. And, the ecopolitical climate of the 1950s ensured the survival of capitalism, which was after all, the end goal of global domination. With the creation of the "clear and present danger" posed by the Soviet Republic to both democracy and capitalism, the United States moved forward with their unilateral agenda, securing global hegemony, and ultimately maintaining preponderant power over an international community. This based in an age of mutual vulnerability, whereby the U.S. was enabled to control the economic, social, and political policies of debtor nations via Marshall Plan loans and NATO. The loans administered and dictated by considerations imposed by the World Bank and International Monetary Fund, such as unrestricted trade and open markets, were critical to development of a global capitalist economy, as they are now. Further, if, and when necessary, enforcement of loan terms was backed by near omnipresence of military might, with U.S. bases and policing established all over the globe. According to Peter Phillips, author of *Giants: The Global Power Elite,* "US military forces are now deployed in 70 percent of the world's nations. US Special Operations Command (SOCOM) has troops in 147 countries, an increase of 80 percent since 2010." [86]

The same tactics used to create the external threat of Communism during the Cold War era, have more recently been successfully introduced as justification for America's "War on Terror," now more appropriately termed perma-war, and the appropriation of public funds for defense purposes. Indeed, as Peter Phillips states in *Giants*,

> The demonization of *others* [is used] as a political justification of permanent war. Understanding permanent war as an economic relief valve for surplus capital is a vital part of comprehending capitalism in the world today. War provides investment opportunity for the Giants and Transnational Capitalist Class (TCC) Elites and a guaranteed return on capital. War also serves a repressive function of keeping the suffering masses of humanity afraid and compliant. [87]

The "evil" men we are now at war with differ geographically and demographically from previous eras, but they threaten the established order and impede capital interests, thus, must be challenged with further militarization by U.S. armed forces, or at least, that is the bill of goods we are handed. And so, it continues, the "Pentagon System," the permanent war mechanism of the unilateral capitalist world order, has been institutionalized globally. Indeed, our nation is engaged in perma-war as Peter Phillips states,

> It is a world of permanent war, whereby spending for destruction requires further spending to rebuild, a cycle that profits the Giants and global networks of economic power. It is a world of drone killings, extrajudicial assassinations, death, and destruction, at home and abroad. [88]

The contradiction between on the one hand, the ideals espoused by America's leaders and the principles upon which America stands and on the other, the ways in which it acts upon those, appears evident. Yet, many true-blue, red-blooded, American citizens continue to believe the mythmakers, the warmongers, the Global Elite.

To the utter amazement of many, history is still in the making as patterns and continuities appear now into the twenty-first century. Social problems do not develop in a vacuum, void of influence, be that influence an economic crisis, a World War, or the fear of nuclear annihilation. Rather, they are directly influenced by and moreover, manipulated within these contexts by a Global Elite. The global economy instituted in the 1950s has become a many-headed monster as we have entered the 21st Century, hungrily devouring all the natural and material resources of the world while poverty grows exponentially, and prosperity is reserved for very few.

An analysis of the structural framework of empire and its workings, and in lived reality for billions globally, demonstrates how an autonomous authority has shaped the behavior of the masses, whether by force, intimidation, dependency, or a combination of the many and varied methods and instruments the Elite have at their disposal to keep the people in their places. Regardless of how the empire manipulates the imperialized, every aspect of life becomes fused with, and subordinated to, the interests of the State or is systematically eliminated as a barrier.

DEMOCRACY

CHAPTER 16

⚖

Democracy

"The liberty of a democracy is not safe if the people tolerated the growth of private power to a point where it becomes stronger than the democratic state itself. That in its essence is fascism: ownership of government by an individual, by a group, or any controlling private power."

—Franklin D. Roosevelt

Democracy, as the political system of American society, is compromised by power dynamics and structural inequalities; thus, in its applications it is merely quasi-Democratic. Power dynamics allow for the Elite members of American society, predominantly white, propertied, heterosexual males, to control and manipulate all other members of society through policy initiatives, legislative regulations, judicial rulings, citizenship rights, and ideologies. Decisions are levied assumedly on behalf of a so-called majority; however, the majority is illusory as indicated in the myriad of interests presented in partisan politics. Partisanship and contested politics serve to advance an Elite agenda.

The United States government, or State, in patriarchal terms is in metaphorical terms, the father to all its citizens. In paternalistic terms, the State acts with the authority of a father over his dependents and in the supposed best interests of his dependents. The father/State determines needs, imposes restrictions on behaviors, distributes punishments and rewards. Quasi-paternalistic notions appear to drive State relations with peoples of the American state, and globally, as evidenced in terms of welfare distribution, immigration law, buildup of the prison-industrial-complex, and policing and control of the geopolitical world. America is paternalistic in that it does offer protection and some measure of acting to meet some of its people's needs. However, wherein paternalism does not require a duty of reciprocity, America does hold its citizens to a reciprocal arrangement in conformance to norms and allegiance to ideologies, as well as, in meeting the injunction to contribute to the state economy as self-supporting.

American citizens are under an implied obligation to the State to assimilate for homogeneity, which includes nationalistic ethos, adherence to individualism, and embracing capitalism. The State's reciprocal duty based in democracy, should then judiciously be, assurance of rights and equality of condition. However, this is not the case with paternalism, nor in the United States. The government is inasmuch the protective father of the nation's integrity against external threats from outsiders, punitive father to all superfluous males as internal threats, and surrogate father to all unmarried welfare mothers and their illegitimate children.

We, the people, as American citizens, and citizens of a global community are at what G. William Domhoff describes as a "critical juncture," an historical moment when it is possible for us to exercise our collective power toward a more egalitarian society. I heartily concur. Dominant class members, the Power Elite, use their structural economic and status power to manipulate policy formation and implementation to dominate the federal government through a bipartisan electoral system. In *Who Rules America: Challenging Corporate and Class Domination*, Domhoff provides an explanation of how capitalists gained their distributive power over labor and along the way, the corporate community and upper class formed a "power elite", effectively ushering all American citizens under the socio-eco-political umbrella of the elitist's agenda. That is, as Domhoff states, the American people are a "polity where there is little or no organized public opinion on specific legislative issues . . . independent of the limits and obfuscations"[89] created by the power elite. There is, then, essentially a mass of acquiescence, quiet acceptance of the status quo by the American people. While we tout our individual freedoms and democratic processes as proofs of American superiority, too many of us do not see the rug being pulled out from underneath us.

American democracy is a treasured institution, a model of government held up to the world audience to be admired and emulated. The principles on which it was founded liberty, equality, and freedom are expressions which speak to every human heart and move every soul. The Declaration of Independence and Preamble to the Constitution of the United States bear witness to our Founding Fathers' intention for America's people. But the truths that were "self-evident," equality of all men, those truths were only so for privileged Elite white men of days-of-old. And, further, intended to "secure the Blessings of Liberty to ourselves and our Posterity" with no mention of women or *others*. Indeed, those rights guaranteed by our creator were never intended for the Native people of the land, nor for newcomers, as immigrants have faced many structural barriers, even having walls built to exclude them. Constitutional amendments were necessary to make room in public space for inalienable rights to be extended to women, Blacks, and numerous other excluded members of this democratic republic. And, now, after having developed American democracy for centuries, we still do not have a united nation that upholds the principles of freedom, equality, liberty, and the pursuit of happiness for all. It is not what the Elite white male founders of America wanted then, and it is not what the Elite white male decision-makers want now. They created an America for them and their heirs, and their heirs have extended the American empire around the world.

CHAPTER 17

The *Strategy Of Tension:* Keeping The Public Pliable And Compliant

"The whole aim of practical politics is to keep the populace alarmed (and hence clamorous to be led to safety) by an endless series of hobgoblins, most of them imaginary."

—H.L. Mencken

Propaganda, public relations, and marketing have been used by the Power Elites to manipulate and control the full consciousness, the minds, bodies, and hearts of a large portion of the American population. A combination of measures has been implemented and maintained to accomplish this feat, including psychological warfare (psyops) and the "strategy of tension"[90] applied not only to populations abroad, but right here in our sovereign nation, neoconservative interventions as counter-revolutionary tools, building solidarity around a nationalist agenda, and group-mind socio-political tactics; all are interwoven into the American cultural arena such that they appear to be just a natural progression of thought processes.

Daniele Ganser, in "The "Strategy of Tension" in the Cold War Period", introduces the concept of strategy of tension, which was deliberately used to target human emotions with the ultimate aim being to keep people in a perpetual state of fear. Further, his discussion of psychological warfare with the U.S. Department of Defense's definition:

> The planned use of propaganda and other psychological actions having the primary purpose of influencing opinions, emotions, attitudes, and behavior of hostile foreign groups in such a way as to support the achievement of national objectives. [91]

Ganser provides insight into how these instruments of control can and have been applied to the American public toward similar ends. The media, both electronic and print, can be implicated in the conditioning of the American psyche to the idea of catastrophe. These forebodings weigh heavily on people's psyches and render them powerless and open to the saving grace of the Father, here taken to mean the national government or State, though the obvious religious associations can be made and argued for as measures of control, as well. Though Ganser concentrates on the "Cold War" era in presenting his argument, the strategy of tension can be readily applied to conditions of external and internal threats during the WWII period and continued into the postwar years in varied form as illustrated by the following interpretation:

The Japanese attack on Pearl Harbor was but a marker along the trajectory in the bitter clash of cultures and capital during the second World War. Propaganda pitting culture against culture set the stage for an internal cleansing on US soil. Caricatures in political cartoons depicting the Japanese as barbarians and beast-like fueled the flames, as did newsreels and print media demonstrating the particularly cruel and barbaric practices of the Japanese Imperial Army.

Fears of Japan's imperialist aspirations operating in America were addressed by informal adoption by both the US and Japanese governments in the Gentlemen's Agreement of 1908. Under the agreement, the US would allow immigrants from Japan to stay in the US, but only wives, children, and immediate family members of those already here would be issued VISAs by Japan. The "photo wives" were admitted based on strict criteria. Upon arriving in America, they were promptly married at the dock and then ushered to shopping areas where they were expected to purchase "white" women clothes, thereby demonstrating their intentions to assimilate. However, these same women were soon marked by what were perceived to be prolific tendencies, interpreted as Japan's imperialist designs realized via these women's uteri. This increased nervousness surrounding Japanese intervention in the continuity of the American, white way of living. Japanese employers were already seen as a threat for what were considered "inappropriate" labor practices; this, in part, because they hired white workers. Now Japanese women with their "uterine nationalism" were attempting to gain ownership of white American's land through proliferation of the race; citizen children could spell doom for white American civilization. This led to further immigration controls, eventually leading to a final exclusionist victory of all Japanese immigrants via the Immigration Act of 1924, banning all Asian immigrants.

These exclusionary tactics could not, however, hold in check the actions of Japanese Americans who might sympathize with their country of origin; at least, those were the rational inclinations of America's leaders. Thus, in the interest of national security, the United States government convinced its already paranoid citizens of the necessity of confining all Japanese, even American citizens, as no chances could be taken with potential Japanese or Axis sympathizers. The US State Department produced and presented to the American public, documentaries demonstrating the "relocation" process and explaining the rationale for the incarceration of tens of thousands of its own citizens.

The US government also used war propaganda apparatus to garner public support of and participation in, the buildup of the "great arsenal of democracy." So effective was this rallying call that for a brief time the country and all its citizens appeared to be united in a common cause, the war effort. Few Americans really understood the complexities faced by the men on the front lines; they simply understood that too many were not coming home alive. The media did a more than adequate job of answering people's curiosity, but more importantly, it directed their consciousness in support of political and military ends. President Roosevelt understood the importance of rallying public support for his short-of-war strategy.

Once the war had come and its toll mounted, a shift of emphasis for the people moved from purely nationalistic concerns to considerations of what this great nation's part should be in restoring international order. By that point, American racial hatred of the Japanese would likely have supported the bombings of Hiroshima and Nagasaki, had the public been informed or consulted, which it was not. After the bombs were dropped the media presented the military maneuver as yet, another demonstration of American superiority and hailed the bombs use. Curiously, presentation by the media of the aftermath of the bombings, of the devastating destruction, and especially of the toll in human suffering and loss of life, was nonexistent. Americans only needed to know that they were victorious; any consideration of US accountability was parlayed into a statement of necessity in ending the war and stopping the loss of lives. US military leaders were aware that terms of surrender were being prepared by the Japanese Imperialist government days prior to the release of "Little Boy" and "Fat Man." However, to establish American dominance in a preponderant show of military might, Japanese civilians were targeted in scorched earth maneuvers in a total war scenario.

Fear seems to be a contributing factor in how our national and local governments respond to crisis as well as instilling everyday paranoia. The crisis of migration into America from the Mexican border has seen migrant activity constructed as threats, thus requiring authorities to enact restrictive laws and implement ever-more punitive measures. In contrast, undocumented immigrants live in constant fear of arrest, fines, jail time, and deportation. They fear losing familial connections and continued economic hardship. American laborers fear losing jobs and benefits to Latinos. They are afraid their children's schools and communities will be "dirtied" by "illegals" and their families. These fears have been manipulated in attempts to garner public support for control measures presented by the Trump administration. Building a wall on the border of our two nations does more than provide a concrete boundary for exclusion; it exemplifies America's ethnocentrism.

This climate of fear, as integral a part of human interaction as it appears to be, is permeable and mutable. If we fail to get around it, we face further separation and division, more exclusion, marginalization, and oppression. Human beings need each other, we are social creatures; we thrive on connection and are mutually dependent on each other to fill basic human needs. We need to take steps to address this climate of fear in opposition to what the government and media keep feeding us about national security, personal security, financial security, etc. Approaching relationships with *others* in a spirit of interdependence with patience, understanding, open communication, and tolerance, fear can and must be overcome. Until every member of society can feel secure, no one will truly be secure, and no amount of fear will protect us.

CHAPTER 18

Ideologies And Institutions: Making Up America's Minds And Capturing Their Hearts

"All things are subject to interpretation, whichever interpretation prevails at a given time is a function of power and not truth."

—Friedrich Nietzsche

The corporate/mainstream media is a tool for creating and maintaining dominant ideologies in favor of capitalism, consumerism, and nationalism, and is a vital instrument to the Elite's success in manipulating the beliefs and controlling the actions of the American people. The Elite contribute to these divisions by controlling public opinion or consciousness. Mass consciousness refers to the degree to which American society internalizes opinions, beliefs, attitudes, and ideologies. Indeed, as Peter Phillips states in *Giants*,

> The transnational media and the PRP, [public relations and propaganda] industry are highly concentrated and fully global. Their primary goal is the promotion of capital growth through the hegemonic psychological control of human desires, emotions, beliefs, and values. [92]

Tools for manipulation of public opinion include censorship, propaganda and public relations, suppression of information, and other methods for control of information. Through the control of information and manipulation of its meaning, America's leaders have molded a pliant mass public consciousness to meet their ends. The public consciousness is manipulated and controlled by relatively small groups of capitalist corporatist men. Differences and divisions for the masses are constructed within these spheres of influence. Keeping the masses separated and uninformed allows the Elite to continue with business, as usual, uncontested and abetted by conformance, complicity, and complacency of the populace. Social injustice is bred and thrives in conditions such as those created and maintained in America's patriarchal, capitalist, quasi-democratic society, and so too, are the divisions that separate and fragment people.

I saw a bumper sticker that read, "If you're not pissed off; you're not paying attention." But what if people are paying attention? What if they are thinking and acting in response to sensory data, they are fed day in and day out by mass mainstream media, such as the news as Truth, and marketing strategies as value-laden? That is, what if people believe and do just as they are expected to? With due consideration given to the idea that the masses of American people are being deliberately manipulated by a mass-media-industrial complex operating with an Elitist agenda, placing profit in mass-markets and global US military domination as prime objectives; is this such a stretch of the imagination?

There is a clear link between democracy and access to information, whereby discussion and opinion-making are techniques not afforded to the masses of American society. Rather, as demonstrated by C.W. Mills, in *The Mass Society*, the public of public opinion is controlled, managed, manipulated, and intimidated by "small circles of men"[93] who have at their grasp "historically unique instruments of psychic management and manipulation"[94] in universal compulsory education and the media of mass communications. Importantly, Mills argues that in a society (such as ours) in which mass mainstream media is manipulated by an Elite group of men, such that the flow of information is dictated within these spheres of influence, democracy cannot truly exist.

The media industry is representative of an institutionalized system of inclusion and exclusion structured in patriarchal systems of domination and control. Further, power as established in our democratic society grants access to the media, to information, in much the same ways as other citizen rights are extended. That is, the distribution of knowledge by the Elite to maintain the status quo, thus, is a matter of power relations. In *Giants: The Global Power Elite,* Peter Phillips explains,

> Corporate media consolidation [has resulted in] managed news by government and PRP firms—often interlocked —including both the release of specific stories intended to build public support as well as the deliberate noncoverage of news stories that may undermine corporate capitalist goals. NATO and power elites are seeking total information control and the elimination of any media challenges to capital's freedom to grow. [95]

Information and communications technologies have done much to provide a more direct route to knowledge-building. However, they have also provided a powerful vehicle through which the mass consciousness of the American people can be, and has been, manipulated and, to a frightening degree, controlled. The dissemination and distribution of information has had powerful implications on the attitudes and belief patterns of the American people as demonstrated herein. The consciousness of the American people has been shaped in support of patterns of exclusion found in patriarchy and advanced in capitalism. Unfortunately, the ability to distinguish what we know from what we think we know and how we know it, contributes substantially to the Power Elite's ability to make us believe or conform. The people of America must now begin building bridges for connection and tearing down psychosocial barriers to inclusiveness. It is up to each of us to question knowledge as based in authority and build our own information base as necessary, to arrive at our own conclusions, even as those may deviate from the masses or lead us ultimately to a disparate end.

CHAPTER 19

American Militarism And Empire: Spreading Democracy or Crushing Rights and Freedoms

"The greatest bulwark of capitalism is militarism".

—Emma Goldman

The military-industrial-media complex infiltrates our lives, our very sense of being, and allows for our complacent acceptance of government propaganda and the politics of domination and violence. There is still evil lurking over there [mid-East], after all; and certainly, with the threats to national security, we should all be willing to allow for just a little more trampling on our rights, as our privacies are compromised yet again, for our own good. And, too, we acquiesce as more of our sons and daughters go invade another country, putting their lives on the line so that we at home may be safe against the never-ending threat of invasion by terrorists. There is nary a trace of a real Democracy in twenty-first century America; nor are the fruits of its existence seen in truth, justice, liberty, or equality. We are all responsible for what happens in our names —*others* in foreign nations will hold us accountable, as a nation, but also as a people, the American people.

In Peter Phillips' and Mickey Huff's essay, "Inside the Military Media Industrial Complex: Impacts on Movements for Peace and Social Justice," the authors expose the Military Industrial Media Complex and insist that we, as American citizens, must resist its efforts and further, how we may continue to search for our own truth(s). The authors suggest addressing "truth emergency"[96] concerns caused by government, military, and corporate sponsored censorship and propagandizing, by developing "collaborative strategies to disclose, legitimize, and popularize deeper historical narratives on power and inequality in the United States."[97] This "media-democracy movement"[98] would expose patterns of power abuse, exact transparency, and expect accountability in an effort to effectively "transform how Americans perceive and defend their world."[99] This is critical in raising consciousness, as well as, helping people to understand how patterns in our beliefs and behaviors, our consciousness (individual and collective) perpetuate patterns of being, and further, allow for power dynamics as based on the politics of domination to continue.

The "necessity to challenge Elite domination"[100] as the authors state, is urgent, as is the need to "unite the people in opposition to the common oppressors"[101]. There is, indeed, a moral dilemma facing Americans and mass ignorance provides little defense as answer to millions of innocent lives lost as U.S. imperialism and military unilateralism continue unabated. Even while we pay homage to our brothers and sisters in arms who have lain their lives on the line in defense of freedoms in our homeland, it is necessary to question the official narratives. The motives of our leaders are masked in rhetoric of freedom and security, but whose freedom and whose security? And, against what enemy? Does homeland security require the militarization of local police forces armed against the people they were commissioned to protect? Patterns and continuities evident in State-sanctioned manipulation and control of foreign nations and their peoples demonstrate a politics of domination and violence in international relations.

Kathryn Temple paints a compelling, emotionally-charged portrait in "Exporting Violence: The School of the Americas, US Intervention in Latin America, and Resistance"[102]. She opens with a graphic depiction of the brutal rape and murder of a 7-year-old, El Salvadoran girl, who despite the dire conditions of her final hours, raised her voice in song. The account is at once horrific and inspirational, and the author draws on the emotional response it elicits as she explains her commitment to direct action and the associated risks. She explains how the El Salvadoran military personnel responsible for the atrocities were trained at the School of the Americas, an "implement of [US] foreign policy," and were funded by U.S. economic and military aid. She considers the dynamics of corporate globalization in terms relative to domestic violence, power and control, and tactics abusers exercise over their victims positing the U.S. government as the abuser and the people of Latin America, the victims. She continues to develop this relationship discussing foreign debt as a tactic for establishing dependency centering on free trade agreements, the International Monetary Fund (IMF), and structural adjustment policies. She illustrates how U.S. government accountability is minimized, deflected with tactics of denial, and blame inverted. Additionally, she argues that the U.S. "war on drugs" is what she refers to as a pretense for manipulating controls over indebted countries, such as Columbia. The picture painted here makes clear how United States involvement, through training military and intelligence personnel at the School of the Americas and providing aid, has offered a position of power enabling the U.S. to manipulate and maintain control over "the world's profit-making resources."

Though the US Army School of the Americas has changed its identity to The Western Hemisphere Institute for Security Cooperation, it still offers training in psychological warfare and interrogation techniques. Indeed, the closure of the U.S. Army School of the Americas was precipitated by legal actions being brought against the institution for its part in the brutal repression of Latin American citizens by their own State agents who were trained by school personnel. There were numerous accusations of crimes against humanity committed by multiple graduates in various capacities. The overriding concern was the U.S. Army School of the Americas had provided the training, training for terror over citizen populations, whereby the people were brutally beaten, raped, tortured, killed, and numerous other human rights violations and atrocities were committed against them.

Cochabamba: Water War in Bolivia is a narrative of injustices heaped upon the people of Bolivia by their State, the courage and resilience the people displayed in standing up and speaking out for their rights, and the continued struggle to make Bolivia a democracy of, for, and by the people. Which with their most recent democratic election, they are closer to than in their nearly 200-year nationhood. The book was written by Oscar Olivera who was one of the most active leaders within the collaborative movement of demonstrations and protests of the water wars in Bolivia. Violent clashes between civilians and Bolivian police occurred over the course of months in early 2000. Factors leading up to this bloody climax were based on neoliberalism and how it came to affect every aspect of the Bolivian people's lives. Within the text of the book Olivera made an appeal to the American people; to become informed and more importantly, to get involved in seeking a global unity for justice. This appeal was made nearly twenty years ago.

These are but two of the published narratives from our global community, other democracies that seek the same quality of life as we do. The difficulties the people of Latin America have suffered are due to U.S. hegemonic aspirations as demonstrated in economic and foreign policies. Neoliberal strategies in play on a global stage are the musings of the Power Elite in transnational corporate terms for a global Capitalist order. The methods and instruments of control are the same, the trends in social problems and poverties are manipulated by the same power dynamics and create the same structural inequalities. The people, our neighbors to the south, are affected by the same triad of power structures, patriarchy, capitalism, and democracy, as we Americans.

Are Americans vain to expect to be treated with dignity and respect by local policing authorities and State entities? The not-so-distant Civil Rights Movement participants and those protesting the wars with Vietnam and Korea met with policing methods to control the civil unrest markedly similar to those observed in cities all over America during Black Lives Matter demonstrations. However, the tools of suppression have increased in mass destructive capacities and increasingly weaponized policing forces and militarized equipment. This buildup seems excessive for potential use against U.S. citizens, yet if not us, then who? It is frighteningly conceivable. Indeed, as Peter Phillips, *Giants,* states,

---

The globalization of Private Military Companies (PMC) operations alongside transnational capital investment, international treaty agreements, and an increasing concentration of wealth in the Trans Capitalist Class (TCC) means that the repressive practices of private security companies abroad will inevitably come home to the United States, the European Union, and other developed nations.[103]

Patterns and continuities in human interaction, especially as seen in Elite manipulation and control of people and the planet for profit are evident here and globally. The problems of our brothers and sisters in distant nations have moved ever closer. Our neighbors across the border are now our neighbors down the street. Their problems are our problems. The connections, rather than the differences, between *us* and *them* have become more apparent as our daily lives are interrupted. Perhaps that is what we need; to be interrupted. A pattern is only a pattern as long, as it continues. A pattern interrupted, must as a matter of course, change. And, in change is possibility.

US Imperialism and military unilateralism are evident in the buildup of the military-industrial-complex, which has paralleled the advance of global capitalism, the prime directive of the Power Elite. Intimidation and force are tried and true methods of manipulation and the masters well-versed in their use. The masses are further manipulated and controlled through mainstream media misinformation, censorship, and propaganda. Economic maneuvers are implemented to increase debt, encourage dependency, and dispossess people from the land and natural resources. The instruments of control and destruction are at the disposal of the Elite, and the world's populations, moreover, disposable masses.

CHAPTER 20

Belonging Denied: Alienation And Anomie In American Culture

"We all construct worldviews that give us a sense of meaning. Mostly it is about belonging to a group and having a sense of identity and purpose."

—Carmen Lawrence

Alienation and anomie have become normalized human responses to lives consumed by capitalism and driven by technological advances. Thus, people are left feeling alone, isolated, and powerless and as if their lives have no meaning or direction. Dissatisfaction with current ways of relating and fitting in, conforming, lead many to consider alternative answers to these confusions. Everyone wants to belong, to fit into a group or to be a part of something according to definitions and socio-cultural constructions as well as, fulfilling a basic human need for connection. Not belonging can lead individuals and groups to be singled-out, labeled, misunderstood, and excluded by larger society. Those individuals who lack a sense of belonging are not alone, rather hundreds of millions of people around the world do not belong, as evidenced in glaring terms, in confinement of immigrant children in U.S. Border Patrol encampments and rejection of asylum-seeking refugees globally. Whole groups of people are marked for compartmentalization, marginalization, and exclusion. The systems of patriarchy, capitalism, and a lack of true democracy create conditions of conflict and competition, rather than cooperation and community. The anomie and alienation of individuals is evidenced in creation of alternative group identities and increased mental illness as discussed herein.

In 2012, Sonoma County's National Alliance on Mental Illness (NAMI) sponsored a FREE speaker-panel event to "share prevention strategies, education, and dissemination of information" on the 10th anniversary of the World Suicide Prevention Day, a world-wide day of awareness. Several "break-out" sessions were offered by facilitators and panelists, the members of which each had some form of mental illness and had contemplated or attempted suicide at least once. The individuals on the panels and millions like them are isolated from society-at-large, their communities, and their families; lonely and alone in a hustle-bustle world that can often seem unforgiving and unyielding. The progress of modern life has wrought a myriad of social ills evident in unemployment, poverty, homelessness, deterioration of the family unit, and concomitant issues which often manifest as mental illness. Is it any wonder that one in four adults in America struggles with some form of mental health issue? And, according to the Suicide Prevention Resource Center, "60-90 percent of suicide victims [youth] have a diagnosable mental illness and/or substance abuse disorder." Thus, for those, the struggle has become one between life and death, or rather, the choice between living and taking one's own life.

What were the circumstances that led these young people in attempts to take their own lives? Did they do it to gain some form of attention? Were they weak-minded? Did they do it out of vindictiveness? What helped them to start on the road to recovery and wellness? These are all questions that were posed by the facilitators to "this panel of courageous individuals" and without equivocation, were answered in personal, meaningful statements. Audience members also posed questions regarding how to reach a loved one battling depression, how to know when a loved one is suicidal, and how to help. The answers surrounded ways of creating a space for the person to feel comfortable talking, for the other to LISTEN (free of judgment), and to ask, "How [I] wanted to be supported."

A prevalent theme among the panel members was lacking a sense of belonging, as demonstrated by their statements, "I had a feeling I wasn't a part of anything," "I didn't fit in . . . I didn't belong, I wasn't a part," "I was just tired of not having anyone care." All panelists spoke to issues coping with depression, having used self-medicating methods of alcohol and drugs, prescribed and otherwise, being in and out of hospital or jail settings, and "hitting brick walls." What helped lead each to progress in recovery was finding "people to feel comfortable to talk to about it," such as counselors "who listened and said nice things," and especially, peer groups wherein "their support and love made me feel I belonged . . . they respected me for who I was."

One of the panelists had been a victim of childhood physical and sexual abuse. Though she "made no connection" to the abuse at the time, the effects of post-traumatic stress disorder escalated to the degree that she "just wanted the pain to stop." She attempted on several occasions to end her life even while "not really wanting to die" and "not wanting to hurt anyone." According to the National Sexual Violence Resource Center, one in three women in America will be the victim of some form of sexual violence in her lifetime, and one in five will be the victim of rape. Additionally, women account for 85 percent of domestic violence victims. This panelist carried the wounds of sexual assault and physical abuse from her childhood in permanent invisible scars and embodiment of her pain. She expressed that she had "a significant degree of recovery" and while "not completely grounded, is grateful to God that life is better."

Another panelist suffered from post-traumatic stress disorder after completing three tours of military service for our country. He is but one of thousands of veterans who suffer in silence the torturous hell of having lived through battle. Veterans represent approximately 11-12 percent of the total homeless population with recent point-of-time counts estimating nearly 40,000 veterans homeless on any given night. Mental health issues from post-traumatic stress as well as social isolation contribute to the numbers who continue to struggle to find a place to belong, a home in their homeland. More concerning than these homeless statistics is the rate of suicides among veterans. Even with adjusted measures at least twenty veterans commit suicide every day in America! And, these figures have not decreased although the number of veterans has decreased by 15%. Further, male veterans are one and one-half times more likely to commit suicide than the general population, while female veterans are over twice as likely to commit suicide than their civilian counterparts. The numbers for female veterans affected speaks to alarming incidences of sexual assault on female military members with the perpetrators, their brothers-in-arms. This young ex-soldier who made it through the lines of combat, nearly succumbed to the ravages of war after returning safely home. He credited the Veterans Administration for helping him "get through," adding "no matter who wears a uniform, they're someone's brother, sister, uncle, nephew, mother, father, and we are on the same roller coaster of life—it's nice to know we are not alone."

Recovery from any illness is a process, one which one panel member compared to education, stating "We're always learning. I'm constantly learning about myself and other people." Another member compared the process to an "endless mountain, one he's climbing every day, one day at a time." The most effective means of beginning the process is developing the ability to communicate, as one panelist stated, "it's made me feel more at ease, takes away the anxiety and shame." The members of the panels were candid and responsive, offering experiential knowledge with dignity and humility, wit, and grace. They offered their stories of struggle, shame, and salvation—they offered hope.

In each human interaction there is a chance for good, for love, for connection, and ultimately, for belonging. However, each time connection is denied, love withheld, or goodness turned bad, hope diminishes. Such is the case for thousands of disenfranchised inner-city and rural community youth; they suffer from alienation as most come from marginalized communities. They live as estranged members from society-at-large by virtue of their birth into an excluded ethnic group, race, or socioeconomic class. Societal expectations, rules, and roles are in confusing and often contradictory spaces in these young people's lives.

We have all seen headlines or heard news announcing yet another innocent life lost due to gang-related violence. In the inner cities of our nation especially, citizens often live in a state of fear created and maintained by local youth, as more and more join and actively participate in gang-related activities. To understand the sociological underpinnings of the youth-gang subculture, informal conversations were held with several currently involved youth gang members (2 males, 2 females) and two young adult males who were no longer affiliated or active. Upon analysis of the content of these conversations, I contend, gang membership offers these youth a quasi-religious (civil) framework for being in the world; herein offered for consideration and clarification.

All the youth as well as, the two young adult males, are members of the lower socioeconomic class in American society and all identified as white. Most were raised in broken families by single parents. While most had extended kinship networks, the majority did not have a close affinity to any family members. Additionally, the youth in these interviews did not perform well in academic or social settings and were, or had been, part of an alternative or extended learning program. Each of these factors are not remarkable in and of themselves, but the factors multiplied as they are here, create exigent circumstances in these youth's lives which contributed to gang affiliation.

The Barbarian Brotherhood (BBH) is an exclusively white-male gang that exists and operates in Lake County, California. None of the juveniles interviewed were actual members of this gang, but they modeled their gang after the BBH. All the participants indicated that they were looking for "a place to belong." The streets are where these kids find a home away from home. To become part of the gang, potential members must be indoctrinated through ritual initiations. For males, the initiation is referred to as a "jump-in" whereby a prospective member is beaten by all other male members. In gangs that accept female members, females are initiated through ritualistic sex, referred to as the "gang-bang." Girls who want to join are expected to "be down" for "giving it up" to all male gang members; in other words, consenting to sex. If they are not "down," they become subject to punishment in the form of a beating by female gang members who are "down." Like many religions, gang membership includes rituals, albeit, in extremely violent and sexualized forms.

Although none of the youth who spoke were affiliated with any organized religion, one of the females stated that she believed in God. The other youth indicated that they did not believe in anything or anyone, but their "homies," other gang members. The gang leader, usually an adult male, introduces the juveniles to the workings of the streets. He teaches them how to steal, deal drugs, and pimp, thereby offering them a means to profit in a world that is otherwise barred from their access. He also determines the system of reward and punishment for all members and gives the orders for enforcement. He leads and controls members initially through fear and intimidation, but in time, members "know" what is expected and what is not accepted. The kids referred to the term "respect" when speaking about their leader. On the flip side of what appears to be a one-sided relationship in favor of the leader, the youth offered explanations for what they receive in return. Members indicated feeling a sense of connection to something bigger than themselves and with this, a sense of "identity." Additionally, gang membership offered them "status" and protection.

In brief, the subculture of juvenile gang activity provides these kids with a sense of hope against the powerlessness they feel; in "working the streets," members can support themselves financially, albeit illegally, through gang methods. Additionally, affiliation with the gang offers members a sense of community in contrast to being alienated by larger society due to socio-economic positioning. Membership in the gang offers these youth a place of belonging, where often they share similar backgrounds and views of the world. Many of the youth identify the gang as "the only family" they have ever had. Further, the gang offers these youth a purpose for their lives, in answer to the anomie, in the "here and now," which is all these kids believe there is. They do not look to the future, because for them, there is no future, only the present moment. Their fatalistic outlook is illustrative of the dynamics of poverty and societal exclusion. They look to a charismatic (often violent) leader for direction and instructions on how to live and thrive in a society that views them as expendable.

America has long been referred to as the "Great Melting Pot" of the world; a nation where peoples from all over the globe, with their differences of ethnicity, language, race, tradition, religion, their cultural identities, all human ingredients come together to create a people, uniquely American. However, America's pot has been left to simmer for too long and the ingredients, the multicultural, multiracial, multiethnic, marginalized peoples of this great nation are boiling over. Attempts at acculturation and assimilation for homogeneity of the masses, as well as a history of systemic abuses visited upon them by Elite white males, supported implicitly and far too often explicitly, by American society have created masses of disenfranchised, dispossessed people. Entire groups of *others* have historically been subject to repression and oppression of their bodies, minds, and souls. Marginalization, exclusion, and compartmentalization based on race, ethnicity, socioeconomic status, age, ability, and/or sexual identity bar individuals and groups from inclusion. Thus, belonging in America is an ever-elusive imagining or created in deviant space where differences are understood and embraced.

PART 3

Moving Toward a New World Vision

CHAPTER 21

⚖️

Speaking Truth To Power: Leveling The Playing Field

*"We live in capitalism. Its power seems inescapable.
So did the divine right of kings. Any human power can be
resisted and changed by human beings. Resistance and change
often begin in art, and very often in our art, the art of words."*

—Ursula K. Le Guin

Through the control of information and manipulation of its meaning, America's leaders have time and again, molded a pliant mass consciousness to meet their ends, and continue to do so even now. As demonstrated throughout this book, the "press" addressed by President Kennedy in 1961 has morphed into a mainstream-media monster. Manipulation of the tools of propaganda, public relations, suppression, and censorship have arguably created a public which is complacent, compliant, and complicit.

> Without debate, without criticism, no Administration and no country can succeed—and no republic can survive—And that is why our press was protected by the First Amendment —the only business in America specifically protected by the Constitution—not primarily to amuse and entertain, not to emphasize the trivial and the sentimental, not to simply give the public what it wants—**but to inform, to arouse, to reflect, to state our dangers and our opportunities, to indicate our crises and our choices, to lead, mold, educate and sometimes even anger public opinion.**
>
> *President John F. Kennedy*
> *Waldorf-Astoria Hotel, New York City April 27, 1961*
> *The President and the Press: Address before the American Newspaper Publishers Association*

Mainstream media and dominant cultural narratives often argue that the poor are the cause of the world's social ills, including overpopulation, increased violence, juvenile delinquency, and crime; they are labeled lazy, opportunistic, criminally (or otherwise) deviant, thus, undeserving of rights and privileges conferred upon citizens by society. Rather, it is my contention that as socially constructed threats to civilized society, numerous and varied control measures are arbitrarily implemented against them to "protect" the dominant class interests and maintain the status quo. Power structures are well served by social stratifications based in differences of class, gender, race, sexuality, ability, religion, and numerous others. Further, these classifications also serve to keep the masses fragmented, isolated, and ignorant. The democratic model can hardly represent an ideal in government when the people are uninformed or purposefully manipulated by propaganda and with misinformation.

To effectively level the playing field for those in poverty and the many affected by the multiple associated manifestations of oppression, it is necessary to challenge current power structures and dominant ideologies. Creating a space for understanding diversity, and further, for opening a dialogue on the subordination of the poor for the privilege of the Elite is imperative. The continuity in this relationship between privilege, profit, and power in creating and maintaining poverty and contributing to the degradation of our planet must be addressed. It is crucial for all whose experiences have been historically marginalized and voices silenced to continue striving to find inlets for expression within the current system.

In addressing the challenges presented by corporate control of mainstream media, we are also provided opportunities to be ingenious and ingenuous in creating new spaces for opening lines of communication and sharing information. We need to create spaces where we can speak freely, outside of the boundaries of current systems; spaces where diversity is celebrated and understanding an inherent part of open discourse. In challenging the dominant systems, ideologies, and narratives, and further, in introducing counterviews of history and alternative visions for human interaction and development, we are in effect, taking the issue to the source, speaking truth to power.

CHAPTER 22

Changing The Dependency Narrative

"Governments have absolutely no interest in self-reliance. It defeats one of the purposes for their existence. They encourage and thrive on dependency. The more of it they sell, the more necessary they are, and the more power and money they need."

—Dan Groat

As demonstrated throughout this text, in personal and political spaces power dynamics operate to create structural barriers to agency. These same dynamics are instrumental in determining how individuals and groups interact with other individuals and groups, how States decide rights and responsibilities relative to citizenship, and even in how we perceive accountability to the living Earth. Research indicates the dynamics of power and structural inequalities are significant barriers to exercise of agency for members of the Poor. However, personal narratives shared by welfare recipients in Lake County, California, demonstrate how single mothers exercise agency in exception to societal barriers. They are aware of how structures, institutions, and ideologies affect their chances for upward economic mobility and self-sufficiency. They are also aware of how institutionalization of ideologies in perceptions, attitudes, and beliefs affect their interaction with larger society as well as, how misperceptions are applied in their interactions by administrators and community members. Rather, than allow these concepts and related effects to keep them in their place, they exercise agency to survive, to challenge dominant narratives, and to strive for self-sufficiency.

In the socio-politico-economic environment every American is enculturated into from birth and considering the embeddedness of dominant ideologies in our consciousness; remaining objective is a difficult task. We come to see each other, especially individuals who act outside of normative scripts, as culpable in their own fates, responsible for their misery, and deserving of little, if any, of society's support. But, as the women demonstrate in constructing their own fates through adversity and often at odds with the welfare system's policies, agency can be exercised, if only in small measure. They are not powerful, but neither are they powerless.

The human spirit is indomitable, as is evidenced in how welfare mothers not only meet but, exceed expectations. Restrictions, invasions of privacy, and punitive measures imposed by welfare agencies, as state agents, effectively control welfare mothers' movements to varying degrees. However, through their exercise of agency, these women defy the odds stacked against them. Without inviting pity or asking forgiveness for their alleged indiscretions, they stand strong against their oppressors in defiance of prevailing notions surrounding their abilities, moral turpitude, and level of decision-making.

I suggest, therefore, that a shift in paradigm has become necessary in how we perceive dependence as applied to welfare mothers. Rather than viewing them as lazy, they are viewed as diligent, rather than opportunistic, they are perceived as self-determined, and rather than irresponsible, they become in public consciousness—resilient and resourceful. These women, single mothers in poverty, who receive or have received welfare benefits; should be looked to for knowledge born of difficult circumstance, wisdom born of pain. They deserve accolades for having the wherewithal not only to survive, but also to thrive and rise above their given station. Rather, than exacting punitive and restrictive measures against them and assuming prejudicial and condescending attitudes toward them, they should be met with respect and encouraged through incentives that support their efforts.

Compassion and understanding need to be applied toward the human beings who live within the confines of situational conditions and exigent circumstances that poverty abides, as these women do. The people of America can and must accept these ideas as a counter-narrative to dominant American misperceptions about welfare mothers and support a change of public consciousness. As a Democratic nation founded on principles of freedom, liberty, and justice, the American state had a duty and an obligation to embrace all its citizens as equals, not least of which its most vulnerable members: single mothers and their children. They are the mothers of millions of children. Have these children been forgotten? Mothers were once touted as the keepers of our nation's conscience, an important role to be sure. In a very real sense these women are the keepers of millions of young minds, spirits, and bodies; and it is their children who suffer the penalties and consequences, or gain the benefits and rewards society imposes or offers. Equality of condition and equality of opportunity must provide the foundation of an interdependent nation with building blocks found in dignity and respect given to every American, regardless of socioeconomic status.

American history has been written based on exceptionalism. These perceptions of an exceptional nation, built by exceptional people, allow for the mythologization of history and perpetuate patterns and continuities in power dynamics and rule by Elites. If the rule calls for welfare recipients to be incapable of change, indifferent to their stations, and insecure in their potentials, then single mothers who receive welfare in Lake County, California, are the exceptions! And, if we are to build our futures upon exceptions, as America has its history, then let it be on the example set by these exceptions—in exception to misguided beliefs, in exception to restricted action, and in exception to limits on Liberty.

CHAPTER 23

Interdependence: The Mutuality of Human Existence

"We can either emphasize those aspects of our traditions, religious or secular, that speak of hatred, exclusion, and suspicion or work with those that stress the interdependence and equality of all human beings. The choice is yours."

—Karen Armstrong

How do we begin restructuring from an individualistic national ethic to one of interdependence? Indeed, how do we begin to construct the foundation for relationships based on mutual dependency in a globalized world? We begin with the recognition that people need people. The whole of human experience does not begin, nor end with the individual. Humans are social creatures and social interaction is where we make connections, to each other, the world, nature, and to our own spirituality. Indeed, it is in relationship with others and identification of ourselves in comparison, that we subconsciously begin positioning for advantage, equality, and/or subordination of self and *others*. So, it is here that we must begin.

At some point or another in each of our lives we have been dependent on someone other than ourselves. Our national ethos of individualism and societal dictates for self-reliance obscures the natural human condition of mutual dependence. In embracing interdependence, we do not diminish the uniqueness of the individual; rather in embracing differences of and between individuals, we celebrate diversity of each and all. In seeking an interdependent community and by extension, State/nation/world, we recognize support of the individual in achieving full development, necessarily elevates the group.

Interdependence develops naturally in times of crisis as can be evidenced in the ways people come together in mutual aid and support, physical, emotional, and financial. Crisis should not have to be a necessary component for people to come together. As we break down constructed barriers to connection with *others,* we effectively create a bridge for interaction, for understanding, and for working toward common goals, together. This is necessary work for the betterment of all. Bridging class divide(s) and working together can create access, allowing for a more equitable distribution of resources. We do not have to take from ourselves in order to give to others. It is possible to care for our own needs and still give due consideration to the needs of others. It is imperative that we operate in a cooperative spirit, empowering ourselves and each other, that is the essence of interdependence. The future of our nation, indeed of the world, is limited not by our compassion, but by our capacity to disrupt the established patterns of American society. In rejecting individualism and embracing interdependence we are being disruptive—can we afford not to?

CHAPTER 24

Applications for Social Justice in Policy and Action

"When we identify where our privilege intersects with somebody else's oppression, we'll find our opportunities to make real change."

—Ijeoma Oluo

First and foremost, capitalism must be regulated by the peoples of the United States, nationally, and by international alliances for the betterment of people and our earth not based on deregulated capital growth. Global capitalism is a well-oiled, meticulously maintained machine, and those who own it, use it to their advantage and the decided disadvantage of everyone and everything else. Sovereignty of nations is mutable, if not nonexistent, in recognition of indebtedness, developmental dependencies, and the globalization of Capitalism. Leaders of governments have little choice, if any, in establishing national goals as policies are dictated for them by the Power Elite, members of the Transnational Capitalist Class (TCC). Indeed, as Peter Phillips, author of *Giants: The Global Power Elite* argues, "The interests of the Global Power Elite and the TCC are fully recognized by major institutions in society. Governments, intelligence services, policymakers, universities, police forces, military, and corporate media all work in support of their vital interests."[104]

Their vital interests are ever-expanding global capital and return on investments. These interests are at odds with an equitable distribution of resources for all peoples of all nations as evidenced in global masses of Poor. Supply-side economics have allowed corporate masters to dictate labor conditions, resource allocation, regulatory policies, and tax initiatives all to their benefit. Meanwhile, as transnational corporations and the owners of capital benefit from lower and lower tax liabilities, the trickle-down effects for the global population are not realized in financial rewards or betterment of living conditions, but in a torrent of social ills. If any appreciable gains are to be made in elevation of the people, then taxation of the Global Elite is a necessary condition.

Policy directives to assist in single mothers' and other low-income members' upward mobility include increased subsidies for higher education, childcare, transportation, housing assistance and increased affordable housing, expanded job training, and entrepreneurial opportunities. Current research supports the primacy of higher education in policy formation, thus an expansion of educational opportunities beyond the level of certificate or Associates degrees must be implemented if any appreciable gains are to be expected for low-income members of the population realization of upward mobility. Entrepreneurial ventures by these individuals should be made available and supported in access to funding, training, networking, and mentorship programs.

Welfare policies have historically been manipulated to coincide with the labor market and capitalist demands. However, if welfare mothers and other low-income citizens are to contribute to the market as self-sufficient members of society and ready consumers, the labor market must compromise. Policies need to be implemented to offer more flexibility in working hours and family leave. The minimum wage needs to be raised to a level sufficient to support families, i.e., a living wage. Additionally, wages for care work for children, disabled, and the elderly should be increased to a living wage.

In "Egalitarianism and the Undeserving Poor," published in The Journal of Political Philosophy, author Richard J. Arneson provides an in-depth analysis and discussion of theories of distributive justice and how notions of individual responsibility and 'deservingness' might be applied to policy initiatives. He concentrates on normative political theory and asserts that theories of justice should be congruous with norms of individual responsibility and deservingness. Theories of deservingness include two aspects, a standard of conduct and an account of responsibility. The standard of conduct is for an individual to act with prudence and within the limits of the law; the exception being the alleged moral obligation for each to be self-supporting. The account of responsibility speaks to the extent to which a person is subject to blame or praise, punishment, or reward, for conformance or lack thereof to the standard. The author introduces a "fine-grained" assessment of deservingness by which an individual might be held to a standard of conduct dependent on the difficulty or personal cost to the individual of conforming. This measure is considered against a coarse-grained deservingness which holds every person to the same degree of conformity. Further, he suggests that even free will is limited or enhanced by helps and hindrances to the ability to exercise it. Arneson argues that deservingness used in policy analysis should be adjusted to assess individual abilities and/or hindrances to their ability to conform to standards of conduct considered normative to which I heartily concur.

Commitments should be made to stricter conformance standards against sexual discrimination by low wage employers and harsher penalties imposed for noncompliance. Infrastructure needs to develop more options for affordable housing as well as increased subsidies to recipients to supplement incomes as housing costs continue to grow. Child support efforts should be increased with wage garnishment as a central component. Punitive measures applied to delinquent fathers need to be reassessed such that they do not introduce barriers to compliance.

Policy analysis and formation should be informed by those who are most directly affected by implementation of welfare laws, the recipients. Single mothers and their children have most at stake, as their very livelihoods depend on the generosity or stinginess of political agents. Additionally, single welfare mothers can offer a wealth of experiential knowledge regarding applied policy and ground-level effectiveness of programs. Thus, participation in planning forums by current and former recipients is essential for fair and just welfare reform.

In "Of Witches, Welfare Queens, and the Disaster Named Poverty," Cassiman argues that the nexus of poverty and trauma provides an opportunity to introduce a rational approach to policy making in the re-conception of social welfare policy as risk prevention. As Cassiman states,

> Failure to acknowledge the devastating nature of poverty, allows the trauma to be perpetuated, and will lead to the intergenerational transmission of poverty, not as a result of inherent cultural deficits, but as a natural result of policy that fails to address the trauma induced by miserly policy responses.[105]

Indeed, because poverty is the direct result of socio-eco-politcal systems dynamics, in developing counter-measures it becomes necessary to politicize the "disaster of poverty" as a counter-narrative to the dominant dependency discourse.

The directives noted are instrumental as supports for single, female, heads-of-households and economically challenged individuals, in general, through policy initiatives as contrasted against restrictions and punitive measures currently imposed. However, to substantially change opportunities for single mothers and other members of the Poor, a restructuring from an individualistic national ethos to one of interdependence is necessary. Society must, in effect, transform its ways of thinking. People must come to understand how patterns and beliefs and behaviors perpetuate patterns of interaction and allow for power dynamics to continue.

CHAPTER 25

Multi-Dimensional Oppositional Consciousness: Bridging Divisions And Developing Alliances

"When feminism does not explicitly oppose racism, and when anti-racism does not incorporate opposition to patriarchy, race and gender politics often end up being antagonistic to each other, and both interests lose."

—Kimberle' Williams Crenshaw

"This land is your land; this land is my land—from California to the New York island; from the Redwood forest to the Gulf stream waters—this land was made for you and me." These are a few of the lyrics written by Woody Guthrie echoing the sentiment of a migrant worker from Oklahoma stopped at the California border by police restricting "vagrants" from crossing state lines during the Depression Era.[107] As a child I remember the song had elicited feelings of national pride for my brothers and myself. We, like so many other Americans, had no understanding of the social context to which it spoke. Ironically, it became an American classic, part of our national social consciousness.

Our social consciousness is molded by culture, shaped by the media, and constructed within the dominant power structure. Collective perceptions, moreover, are manipulated in support of the status quo. These perceptions allow for patterns and continuities manifested in privilege and oppressions. The plight of the Poor illustrates how prevailing ideological beliefs and related structural inequalities create and maintain poverty. To effectively eliminate poverty and the multiple concomitant manifestations of oppression, it is necessary to challenge "dominant collective beliefs and reframe collective perceptions of social relationships in terms of injustice and inequality."[108] Structural inequalities and power dynamics can be vetted by operating anti-poverty movements from a multi-dimensional oppositional consciousness platform. The manifestation of this consciousness has led to the development of what is now being termed the Global Social Justice Movement.

The multi-dimensional oppositional consciousness platform model was introduced by groups forming coalitions for AIDS intervention and advocacy, when members of various groups recognized overlapping and interwoven issues and that often, many had faced varying degrees of oppression in multiple forms simultaneously. In "The Making of Oppositional Consciousness," Jane Mansbridge defines oppositional consciousness as:

> An empowering mental state that prepares members of an oppressed group to act to undermine, reform, or overthrow a system of human domination ... Fueled by righteous anger over injustices done to the group and identifying a specific

> group as causing and . . . benefitting from those injustices and seeing certain actions of the dominant group as forming a system that advances the interests of the dominant group.[109]

It is necessary to challenge dominant perceptions and structures constructed by Elite members of society, as well as, to unite people in opposition. Therefore, upon identifying Elite corporate capitalists as the dominant group within an interlocking system of patriarchy, capitalism, and faux democracy, I argue for adopting a multi-dimensional oppositional consciousness toward those ends.

Stockdill suggests utilizing the four following strategies to effectively organize for multi-dimensional oppositional consciousness: constructive dialogue, empowerment initiatives, community embeddedness, and utilization of Indigenous cultural traditions. Further, utilizing these four strategies, three broad outcomes have been realized: collective consciousness, individual empowerment, and collective action.[110]

Understanding, compassion, and empathy will lead us to this meeting of minds and hearts in a multi-dimensional oppositional consciousness space. Within this space it is paramount to create a vision of the world we want—what we are For. The ideas we are For, are the combined visions of a multi-cultural, multi-racial, multi-ethnic, humanistic new world—a world where the masses think in fully developed or evolved consciousness and move with full agency—a world that is pro-equality, pro-diversity, pro-feminine, and pro-self-actualization—a world where black lives matter, where the elderly, women, our youth, and children are valued, where the earth is revered, and animals respected. Adopting a human rights framework and platform for engagement and action is fundamental to this work. To change consciousness, we must first engage consciousness.

CHAPTER 26

Human Rights: A Framework For Action And Interaction

"We can disagree and still love each other unless your disagreement is rooted in my oppression and denial of my humanity and right to exist."

—James Baldwin

The dynamism of U.S. economic and political agendas promotes individualistic and fundamentalist expressions of power that must be challenged and dismantled. As the proffers to the poor shrivel, the return on investments in and of crisis, work in the Elite's decided favor. The global Power Elite have made a royal mess of things pushing a capitalist agenda as a global economic solution for all the world's ills. What arrogance. With profit as the bottom line, ecological degradation and human suffering necessarily become simply, the cost of doing business in a global environment.

Recent movements in the United States against police brutality, in defense of black lives, and for justice are reminiscent of similar movements for civil rights in the 1960s. Patterns and continuities in the brutal treatment of peoples of color, the Poor, and Indigenous peoples are evident in every corner of the globe. The global demonstrations in support of Black Lives Matter are acts of solidarity and expressions of unity. Our global neighbors, the people distant as they may seem, are not our enemies. They understand multiple oppressions heaped upon the backs of Blacks because their people have suffered similarly through neglect and abuse.

The global community of *others* recognize themselves in America's people of color, Indigenous peoples, and other marginalized groups—in our struggles, our frustrations, our anger, and our pain. This shared sense of oppression, the parallels in lived experience, in shared needs, in humanness; help us to make connections to the rest of the world, as well as illuminate like oppressions under common oppressive systems. Additionally, it connects neglect and abuse of citizens of America with abuses of peoples abroad perpetrated in the interests of US Imperialism and global capitalism. Here is where we share common ground, and it is our starting place for change.

The United Nations introduced *The Universal Declaration of Human Rights* in December of 1948, a proclamation of a "common standard of achievement for all peoples and all nations"[111] for "recognition of the inherent dignity and of the equal and inalienable rights of all members of the human family."[112] Additionally, at the 2016 UN Millennium Summit, Sustainable Development Goals (SDGs) were introduced with completion dates set between now and 2030. These goals were for meeting basic human needs while offering respect and dignity.

Further, in December of 1966 the United Nations General Assembly introduced for signatures the International Bill of Human Rights in two documents, the International Covenant on Civil and Political Rights and the International Covenant on Economic, Social, and Cultural Rights. The purpose of the treaty was to provide some sense of protection and security to the guiding principles of state accountability for meeting basic human rights of State's citizens, emboldened and backed by the signatures and ratification of over 170 countries' leaders.

Curiously, the leaders of the United States of America, except for President Jimmy Carter in 1977 have found supporting fundamental rights for all its citizens outside of the scope of purview, as each administration continues to deem ratification by Congress an inconvenience. Are we to assume that our government does not place value in its citizenry? To deny international support of rights to an adequate standard of living, including the right to food and the right to housing, basic needs for human existence, leaves one to wonder.

In the implied social contract between our government and each of us, we might assume reciprocity between the parties. Are we not to understand that we owe a duty to our nation, just as it most assuredly owes one to each of us? Indeed, the idea of mutual benefit underlies a reciprocal arrangement. We are citizens of the greatest nation in history, unsurpassed in scientific advancements and human capital. That is the face we show the world. And, to be fair, Americans, the peoples, are adventurous and fearful, achievement-oriented and laissez-faire, strong and weak; truly an eclectic mix of the best and the worst, contradictions in human nature and paragons of human potentials. However, it is not the American people at issue, but the Elite who set the rules, call the shots, and rack up the gains.

The American people are being called upon to join the rest of the world's peoples in an impassioned cry to the world's leaders for peace, for justice, for fairness, for equality. The least of us deserves to be afforded basic human decency as demonstrated in respect and dignity no less than the greatest of us. It is incumbent upon each of us to seek these goals for all of us. Those among us who can speak, must speak, and hold those in power responsible and accountable. Human rights are intrinsic to each of us—are we not each human?

Conclusion

"If human beings are perceived as potentials rather than problems, as possessing strengths instead of weaknesses, as unlimited rather than dull and unresponsive, then they thrive and grow to their capabilities."

— Barbara Bush, former First Lady of the U.S

Structural inequalities and their effects on an individual's agency can be understood in the form of a metaphor, as environmental influences introduced to a flowing River. The flow of the river is constricted by boulders/structural barriers, smaller rocks/institutional measures, stones/societal controls, pebbles/internalized constructs, and sediment/environment. Each layer of rock binds movement of the water until eventually the river is dammed up, the water no longer flowing but stilled. As applied to human development then; structural barriers, institutional measures, societal controls, internalized constructs, and our environments act in tandem to constrict the movements of individuals and groups in the larger society.

Control is maintained by dividing and isolating people and by keeping them ignorant and without the ability to exercise full agency, essentially robbing them of their freedoms: to speak, to gather, to choose, to act, and ultimately, to be (exist). Power by, of, and for the people will only be possible when people stop allowing themselves to be manipulated, become informed, and then stand up, speak out, and act out if/when necessary. This book is meant to challenge people to seek truths beyond what they are told by authorities, the official narratives, move around the boundaries in their own minds, and seek ways to find common ground for saving our world. That is what great leaders do, at their own peril, for the sake of all humanity and the planet; it is what we all must do if we are to break the system down and start anew. A new way of thinking, acting, knowing, and feeling is necessary to heal America's (and, in turn, the world's) social, economic, and political woes. And, with a little luck, maybe the world's people will join us, not out of fear, but despite it—in abiding faith and hope for a brighter, more equitable future for the many and the one, many peoples—one race, the human race. As stewards of the planet, we have an obligation, a responsibility, to protect the planet and all its inhabitants.

The complex web of capitalism in a world economy has caused a plethora of social ills as seen in increased global poverty, millions of invisible migrant workers, migration patterns, and the feminization surrounding these issues. There is a revolution upon us, a revolution for life; it is simultaneously being waged in defense of the environment, civil rights, women's rights, children's rights, reproductive rights, and animal rights.

An international dialogue against the multiple dimensions of oppression has begun. It is a dialogue of millions of voices, and it will not be silenced —it will be heard. In idleness and ignorance, we have contributed to our own demise. The desire for a new civil society has become a necessity. Continuation of the human race and that of the very planet hang in the balance. The time for coming together, standing together, and speaking in one voice as a collective, is now. In rejecting the bill of goods, we have been offered by the Global Power Elite; we begin taking back our power —the power of the people, by the people, and for the people.

As we each individually stand and speak from our place of knowing, we contribute to understanding. If we then listen to each other's stories we may come to understand each other. In this place of understanding, we may share space with compassion and empathy, rather than with hearts and minds filled with fear, anger, hatred, disgust, pity, and other emotions that keep us separated. Perhaps, in this space of understanding, we may move forward together, valuing and caring for all.

Today, Americans face what much of the world population has already experienced, a social and economic crisis that threatens us at our core. Hundreds of millions of people, single mothers, peoples of color, and Indigenous peoples are not afforded human dignity, self-determination, or respect. No one is unaffected by the associated effects of poverty, except perhaps the Power Elite. The victims as always are innocent and forgotten. They are not faceless strangers. They are our women and children, elderly, disabled, Indigenous, peoples of color, and young adults. They depend on us and we on them. There is no longer a convenient separation of *us* and *them*, they are us, and we are one. We are many peoples in and of one nation, and part of one world. We can create a new world from a shared vision—a world where compassion and empathy lead and division and hatred are subsumed by understanding and caring. It is ultimately up to us, each and all, we the people, to create the world we want. We must find common ground to come together and move forward toward a new world vision, in peace and with love for our sisters and brothers. We can and must shift the power in our favor such that we win, no one loses, and we all decide. Power to the People!

Glossary of Terms

Abhorrible: Conditions which are harsh, intolerable, unsafe, dehumanizing, and/or inhumane.

Acculturation: Process by which a dominant culture of an area indoctrinates other cultures for assimilation.

Agency: A person's ability to act with free will in moving through and interacting with their environments.

Alienation: Feelings of separateness or isolation from one's environment.

Anomie: Feelings of lack of purpose.

Assimilation: Process by which cultures become homogeneous.

Belonging: Being or feeling accepted as part of a relationship.

Citizen: A member of society or State/government entitled to rights, benefits, and protections by society or the State.

Civilizational: Relating to civilization.

Colonialization: Process by which one State dominates over another, includes political, economic, and social subjection and subjugation of the people.

Conditionalities: terms under which the nations must operate for fiscal responsibility which often include austerity measures.

Developmental Citizenship: Citizen rights as granted by dominant power structures within and between States.

Compartmentalization: Method by which citizens are classified based on belonging determined as based on contribution and/or threat to civilization.

Culture of Dominance: A culture that accepts domination and violence as implicit to maintenance of civilization.

Elite/Power Elite: A relatively small group of mostly white, extremely wealthy, highly connected, and ideologically same, men. Not all extremely wealthy or high-status individuals are elite.

Enculturation: Process by which an individual acquires their own culture.

Faux-Democracy/Quasi-Democratic: Democracy that is false or partial in meeting the principles, activities, values, duty, and responsibilities to the people.

Hegemony: Dominance by one group over another, group classification based on gender, race, status, education, etc.

Homogeneity: Similarity in ideology, tradition, custom, language, and other markers of culture.

Ideologies: Dominant beliefs and attitudes adopted by society members as norms, creeds, ethos.

Imperialism: Intentional expansion of a State for power over and control of resources, including natural and man-made, of foreign nations.

Inculcate/Inculcations: Forced learning, including academic, civil, ideological, and religious.

Institutionalization: Ways in which norms, beliefs, attitudes, and behaviors are established, maintained, and perpetuated.

Interdependence: Ways in which people depend on other people to meet their own needs and the needs of others.

Legitimation: Processes applied to ideas to achieve acceptance or authority by society members.

Marginalization: Compartmentalization applied to groups in provisional access to rights and exclusion from entitlements and protections.

Medicalization: Applying medicalized understandings to human development and behavior.

Multilateral: Agreements and actions between multiple States/Nations. Sovereignty of States is malleable and mutable.

Mythologization: History biased in favor of the dominant power at any given time.

Neo-Colonialism: Modern forms of State control of subjugated State's peoples and resources.

Neo-Liberalism: Elite policies for the advancement of Capitalism and the free market, favoring privatization and against State spending or regulation of Capitalism. However, support State intervention in population control tactics and measures to minimize social spending.

Oppositional Consciousness: Conscious disagreement with or opposition to dominant ideas.

Others: Any individual or group outside of your normal scope of interaction with family and friends, especially those you believe, expect, or understand to be different in race, gender, religion, sexuality, age, ability, etc., etc.

Paradigm: A model of dominant norms; patterned ways of believing and acting; historical continuities can be demonstrated.

Pathologize: To make to appear ill or diseased, thus in need of intervention for correction. Can be applied as defect or perceived deficit in mind, body, or behavior.

Paternalistic: State relationship with citizens as compared to a father and dependent; the State subordinates the people but is conceived of as acting in the people's (subjugated) best interests.

Patriarchal Bargaining: Methods individuals and groups use to elevate, if only in perception, their own status in comparison to others.

Patriarchy: Social system of Western society and most modern societies globally. Hierarchal classification system whereby a person's social position is determined based on sex, gender, race, class, ability, age, and other markers of difference. Male-dominated society.

Provisional Citizenship: Citizens allowed only provisional access to rights, entitlements, and protections; exclusion is implied.

Racialization: Racist constructions in science and medicine.

Scientific Racialism: The use of scientific research to create difference based on race, gender, or other constructed classification.

Self-actualization: Acting in full consciousness. Self-worth, self-dignity, self-determination, and self-respect are key elements.

State: Nation or government structure having control over people and resources within distinguished borders.

Stigma: Internalized negative effect of labels, stereotypes, and prejudices.

Structure(s)/System/Network: Organizations of power, which either elevate or subjugate individuals/groups.

Unilateralism: Actions taken for the benefit of one party.

Endnotes

[1] Harrington, *The New American Poverty*, 81-84.
[2] Ibid, 71.
[3] Ci, "Agency and Other Stakes of Poverty," 133.
[4] Collins, "Learning from the Outsider Within," S22.
[5] Ibid, S19.
[6] Ibid, S19.
[7] Ibid, S29.
[8] Ibid, S30.
[9] Carastathis, "The Concept of Intersectionality in Feminist Theory," 308.
[10] Cassiman, "Of Witches, Welfare Queens, and the Disaster Named Poverty," 57.
[11] Ibid, 53.
[12] Ibid, 53.
[13] Ibid, 54.
[14] Wray, "Three Generations of Imbeciles Are Enough," 174.
[15] Molina, "Medicalizing the Mexican," 27.
[16] Ibid, 30.
[17] Ibid, 33.
[18] Cronon, *Changes in the Land*, 53.
[19] Ibid, 20, 65.
[20] Ibid, 52.
[21] Ibid, 63.
[22] Ibid, 68.
[23] Ibid, 56.
[24] Ibid, 77.
[25] Harrington, The New American Poverty, 171, 192.
[26] Phillips, Giants, 161, 162.
[27] Harrington, *The New American Poverty*, 188, 189.
[28] Ibid, 189.
[29] Ibid, 189.
[30] Ibid, 192.
[31] Ibid, 192.
[32] National Resource Center on Children and Families of the Incarcerated
[33] Empty Cages Collective, "What Is the Prison Industrial Complex," n.d.
[34] Harrington, *The New American Poverty*, 188, 189.
[35] Cassiman, "Of Witches, Welfare Queens," 60.
[36] Broussard, "Research Regarding Low-Income Single Mothers' Mental and Physical Health," 443-451.
[37] Harrington, The New American Poverty, 193.

[38] Jeffreys, "Making Up Is Hard to Do," 113.
[39] Ibid, 120.
[40] Bordo, "Beauty (Re)Discovers the Male Body," 173.
[41] Kilbourne, "The More You Subtract, the More You Add," 135. Quote from Goodman, E. "The Culture of Thin Bites Fiji teens." *Boston Globe*, May 27, 1999.
[42] Ibid, 135.
[43] Garland-Thomson, "Feminist Theory, the Body, and the Disabled Figure," 156.
[44] Ibid, 161.
[45] Kilbourne, "The More You Subtract, the More You Add," 132.
[46] Ibid, 134.
[47] Garland-Thomson, "Feminist Theory, the Body, and the Disabled Figure," 161.
[48] Ibid, 161.
[49] Knopf-Newman, "Public Eyes," 238, 239.
[50] Ibid, 239.
[51] Asian Communities for Reproductive Justice, "Reproductive Justice," 229.
[52] Chernik, "The Body Politic," 141.
[53] Ibid, 142.
[54] Asian Communities for Reproductive Justice, "Reproductive Justice," 230.
[55] Bordo, "Beauty (Re)Discovers the Male Body," 174.
[56] Phillips, Giants, 27.
[57] Ibid, 62.
[58] Ibid, 29.
[59] Ibid, 185.
[60] Ibid, 34.
[61] Ibid, 34.
[62] Harrington, The New American Poverty, 12, 55, 64.
[63] Ibid, 10-12.
[64] Ibid, 10-12.
[65] Ibid, 10-12.
[66] Klein, *The Shock Doctrine*, 62.
[67] Ibid, 10, 94.
[68] Ibid, 22.
[69] Ibid, 9.
[70] Ibid, 23.
[71] Ibid, 6, 377.
[72] Falk, "Global Ambitions and Geopolitical War," 120.
[73] U.S. Const. amend. I.
[74] Klein, *The Shock Doctrine*, 14.
[75] Ibid, 419.
[76] Pauwels, *The Myth of the Good War*, 16.
[77] Ibid, 16, 17.
[78] Ibid, 10.
[79] Ibid, 12.

[80] Ibid, 12.
[81] Ibid, 25.
[82] Ibid, 14.
[83] Ibid, 78.
[84] Ibid, 56.
[85] Ibid, 66.
[86] Phillips, *Giants*, 221.
[87] Ibid, 223.
[88] Ibid, 227.
[89] Domhoff, *Who Rules America*, 193.
[90] Ganser, "The 'Strategy of Tension' in the Cold War Period," 82.
[91] Ibid, 82-83.
[92] Phillips, *Giants*, 300.
[93] Mills, "The Mass Society," 317.
[94] Ibid, 310.
[95] Ibid, 295.
[96] Phillips and Huff, "Inside the Military Media Industrial Complex," 3.
[97] Ibid, 11.
[98] Ibid, 10.
[99] Ibid, 11.
[100] Ibid, 18.
[101] Ibid, 17.
[102] Temple, "Exporting Violence," article no longer available.
[103] Phillips, *Giants*, 260.
[104] Ibid, 158.
[105] Cassiman, "Of Witches, Welfare Queens, and the Disaster Named Poverty," 59.
[106] Ibid, 64.
[107] Harrington, *The New American Poverty*, 151.
[108] Stockdill, "Forging a Multidimensional Oppositional Consciousness," 204.
[109] Mansbridge, "The Making of Oppositional Consciousness," 4-5.
[110] Stockdill, "Forging a Multidimensional Oppositional Consciousness," 215.
[111] UN General Assembly, "Universal Declaration of Human Rights," 217 (III) A, preamble.
[112] UN General Assembly, "Universal Declaration of Human Rights," 217 (III) A, preamble.

Bibliography

Anderson, Glenda. "Poverty Pervasive in Lake County." *The Press Democrat.* February 24, 2015. http://www.pressdemocrat.com/news/3440394-181/poverty-pervasive-in-lake.

Appelbaum, Lauren. "The Influence of Perceived Deservingness on Policy Decisions Regarding Aid to the Poor." *Political Psychology* 22, no.3 (2001): 419-442.

Appleby, Joyce., Hunt Lynn, and Jacob, Margaret. *Telling the Truth about History.* New York: W.W. Norton & Company, Inc., 1994.

Armbruster, Ben. "Fox Pundit Says Women in the Military Should 'Expect' to Be Raped." *ThinkProgress,* February 13, 2012. http://thinkprogress.org/security/2012/02/13/424239/fox-women-military-expect-raped/?m

Arneson, Richard. "Egalitarianism and the Undeserving Poor." *The Journal of Political Philosophy 5, no.* 4 (1997): 327-350.

Asian Communities for Reproductive Justice. "Reproductive Justice: Vision, Analysis, and Action for a Stronger Movement." In *Women's Lives: Multicultural Perspectives*, edited by Gwyn Kirk and Margo Okazawa-Rey. (227-230). New York:McGraw-Hill, 2007.

Badkhen, Anna. "Iraq: The Hidden Crime of Rape." FRONTLINE World. February 2, 2012. http://www.pbs.org/frontlineworld/stories/pakistan802/video/video_index_baghdad.html

Barnes, Sandra. "A Case Study of the Working Poor Single Mother Experience: An Analysis of the Structure Versus Agency Discourse." *Journal of Poverty* 12, no. 2 (2008):175-200.

Bederman, Gail. 'Teaching Our Sons to Do What We Have Been Teaching the Savages to Avoid"; G. Stanley Hall, Racial Recapitulation, and the Neurasthenic Paradox." In *Manliness and Civilization: A Cultural History of Gender and Race in the United States, 1880-1917.* (77-120). Chicago: University of Chicago Press, 1995.

Block, Fred, Cloward, Richard, Ehrenreich, Barbara, and Piven, Frances Fox. *The Mean Season: Attack on the Welfare State.* New York:Pantheon Books, 1987.

Bonsignore, Antoinette. "The Military's Rape and Sexual Assault Epidemic." Truthout. April 3, 2011. https://truthout.org/articles/the-militarys-rape-and-sexual-assault-epidemic/

Bordo, Susan. "Beauty Rediscovers the Male Body." *The Male Body: A New Look at Men in Public and Private.* (129-177). New York: Farrar, Straus and Giroux, 1999.

Brenner, Johanna. "Feminization of poverty and comparable worth: Radical versus liberal approaches." In *The Social Construction of Gender,* edited by Judith Lorber and Susan Farrell, 104-118. Newbury Park, CA: SAGE Publications, Inc., 1991.

Broussard, C. Anne. "Research Regarding Low-income Single Mothers' Mental and Physical Health: A Decade in Review." *Journal of Poverty* 14, (2010): 443-451. https://doi.org/10.1080/10875549.2010.518003.

Carastathis, Anna. "The Concept of Intersectionality in Feminist Theory." *Philosophy Compass* 9, no. 5 (2014):304–314. https://doi.org/10.1111/phc3.12129.

Cassiman, Shawn. "Of Witches, Welfare Queens, and the Disaster Named Poverty: The Search for a Counter-narrative." *Journal of Poverty* 10, no. 4 (2006): 51-66. https://doi.org/10.1300/J134v10n04_03.

Chernik, Abra Fortune. "The Body Politic." In *Women's Lives: Multicultural Perspectives*, edited by Gwyn Kirk and Margo Okazawa-Rey. (140-144). New York: McGraw-Hill, 2007.

Chunn, Dorothy E. and Gavigan, Shelley A.M. "Welfare Law, Welfare Fraud, and the Moral Regulation of the 'Never Deserving' Poor." *Social Legal Studies* 13, no. 2 (2004): 219-243. http://sls.sagepublcom/cgi/content/abstract/13/2/219

Ci, Jiwei. "Agency and Other Stakes of Poverty." *The Journal of Political Philosophy* 21, no. 2 (2013):111-136.

Collins, Patricia Hill. *Black Sexual Politics: African Americans, Gender, and the New Racism*. New York:Routledge, 2004.

Collins, Patricia Hill. "Learning from the Outsider Within: The Sociological Significance of Black Feminist Thought." *Social Problems* 33, no. 6 (1986): S14-32. https://doi.org:10.2307/800672.

Cronon, William. *Changes in the Land: Indians, Colonists, and the Ecology of New England*. New York:Hill & Wang. 2003. *Declaration of Independence*. Paragraph 2, (1776)

Domhoff, G. William. *Who Rules America: Challenging Corporate and Class Domination*. New York:McGraw Hill. 2010.

Duncan, Greg and Magnuson, Katherine. "The Long Reach of Early Childhood Poverty." *Pathways: A Magazine on Poverty, Inequality, and Social Policy*, (Winter 2011): 22-27. https://inequality.stanford.edu/sites/default/files/Pathways Winter11.pdf

Ellwood, David T. *Poor support: Poverty in the American family*. New York: Basic Books, Inc.1988.

Ely, James W. "'There are Few Subjects in Political Economy of Greater Difficulty': The Poor Laws of the Antebellum South." *American Bar Foundation Research Journal* 10, no. 4. (1985): 849-879.

Empty Cages Collective: Organizing and Action Against the Prison Industrial Complex. N.D. "What Is the Prison Industrial Complex?" Accessed 12/2016. http://www.prisonabolition.org/what-is-the-prison-industrial-complex

Falk, Richard. "Global Ambitions and Geopolitical War: The Domestic Challenge." In *9/11 and American Empire: Intellectuals Speak Out*, edited by David Ray Griffin and Peter Dale Scott, 117-127. Northampton:Olive Branch Press, 2007.

Feagin, Joe R., & Vera, Hernan. *Liberation Sociology*. Denver:Westview Press. 2001.

Fox Piven, Frances. & Cloward, Richard. *Regulating the Poor: The Functions of Public Welfare*. New York:Vintage Books. 1993.

Gaddis, John Lewis. *We Now Know: Rethinking Cold War History*. New York:Oxford University Press. 1998.

Ganser, Daniele. "The 'Strategy of Tension' in the Cold War Period." In *9/11 and American Empire: Intellectuals Speak Out*, edited by David Ray Griffin and Peter Dale Scott, 79-99. Northampton:Olive Branch Press, 2007.

Garland-Thomson, Rosemarie. "Feminist Theory, the Body, and the Disabled Figure." In *Women's Lives:Multicultural Perspectives*, edited by Gwyn Kirk and Margo Okazawa-Rey. (156-163). New York:McGraw-Hill, 2007.

Gibbs, Nancy. "Sexual Assaults on Female Soldiers: Don't Ask, Don't Tell." TIME. March 8, 2010. http://content.time.com/time/subscriber/article/0,33009, 1968110,00.html

Hamilton, C. J. "Foreign and Colonial Systems of Poor Law Relief." *The Economic Journal* 21, no. 81 (1911): 156-58. doi:10.2307/2222097.

Harrington, Michael. *The Other America: Poverty in the United States*. New York: Touchstone 1981.

Harrington, Michael. *The New American Poverty*. New York:Penguin Books. 1987.

Hays, Sharon. *Flat Broke with Children: Women in the Age of Welfare Reform*. New York: Oxford University Press. 2003.

Hirsch, Thomas, Rank, Mark, and Kusi-Appouh, Dela. "Ideology and the Experience of Poverty Risk: Views About Poverty Within a Focus Group Design." *Journal of Poverty* 15, no. 3 (2011):350-370. doi: 10.1080/10875549.2011.589680.

Institute for Research on Poverty. *"What are Poverty Thresholds and Poverty Guidelines?"* (2013). https://www.irp.wisc.edu/resources/what-are-poverty-thresholds-and-poverty-guidelines

Jeffreys, Sheila. "Making Up Is Hard to Do." In *Beauty and Misogyny: Harmful Cultural Practices in the West*, (107-127). New York:Routledge, 2005.

Kandiyoti, Deniz. "Bargaining with Patriarchy." In *The Social Construction of Gender* edited by Judith Lorber and Susan Farrell, 104-118. Newbury Park: SAGE Publications, Inc. 1991.

Katz, Michael B. *In the Shadow of the Poorhouse: A Social History of Welfare in America*. New York:Basic Books. 1996.

Katz, Sheila. "TANF's 15th Anniversary and the Great Recession: Are Low-Income Mothers Celebrating Upward Economic Mobility?" *Sociology Compass 6, no. 8* (2012): 657- 670. doi: 10.1111/j.1751-9020.2012.00479x

Katz, Sheila. "'Give Us a Chance to Get an Education': Single Mothers' Survival Narratives and Strategies for Pursuing Higher Education on Welfare." *Journal of Poverty,* 17, (2013): 273- 304. doi: 10.1080/10875549.2013.804477.

Kennedy, David M. *Freedom From Fear: The American People in Depression and War, 1929-1945.* New York:Oxford University Press. 1999.

Kilbourne, Jean. "The More You Subtract, the More You Add." In *Women's Lives: Multicultural Perspectives,* edited by Gwyn Kirk and Margo Okazawa-Rey. (132-139). New York:McGraw-Hill, 2007.

Klein, Naomi. *The Shock Doctrine.* Harlow, England: Penguin Books. 2008.

Knopf-Newman, Marcy Jane. "Public Eyes." In *Women's Lives:Multicultural Perspectives,* edited by Gwyn Kirk and Margo Okazawa-Rey. (237-247). New York: McGraw-Hill, 2007.

Lake County Comprehensive Economic Development Strategy (CEDS). [Data File]. (2016). http://www.co.lake.ca.us/Assets/Economic+Development/Docs/2016+CEDS.pdf

Lendman, Stephen. "Unaccountable: Private Military Contractor Abuses." January 01, 2012.Stephen Lendman. https://stephenlendman.org/2012/01/unaccountable-private-military/

Lewis, Julie R. "Against All Odds: How Welfare Recipients in Lake County, CA Exercise Socio-Economic Agency." MA thesis, Sonoma State University, 2016.

Lewis, Julie R. "American Psychological Warfare: Psycho-political Power Plays in the American People's Aiding and Abetting Proponents of the 'War on Terror'." *Sonoma State Star* 69, no. 3 (Sept. 10-16, 2012): 3.

Lewis, Julie R. "Sonoma County Alliance Offers Hope for People with Mental Illnesses." *Sonoma State Star* 69, no. 4 (Sept. 17-13, 2012): 9.

Mackey, Howard "The Operation of the English Old Poor Law in Colonial Virginia." *The Virginia Magazine of History and Biography* 73, no. 1 (1965): 29-40. http//www.jstor.org/stable/4247080

Mallon, Anthony J. and Stevens, Guy V.G. "Making the 1996 Welfare Reform Work: The Promise of a Job." *Journal of Poverty* 15, no. 2 (2011):113-140. doi: 10.1080/10875549-2011.563169.

Mansbridge, Jane. "The Making of Oppositional Consciousness." In *Oppositional Consciousness:The Subjective Roots of Social Protest* edited by Jane Mansbridge and Aldon Morris, 1-19. Chicago:The University of Chicago Press. 2001.

Marger, Martin. *Social Inequality: Patterns and Processes.* Michigan State University: McGraw-Hill Higher Education. 2002.

McCormack, Karen. "Resisting the Welfare Mother: The Power of Welfare Discourse and Tactics of Resistance. *Critical Sociology* 30, no. 2, (2004):335-383. doi: 10.1163/156916304323072143.

McLarin, Kimberly J. "For the Poor, Defining Who Deserves What." *The New York Times,* Sept. 17, 1995.

Mills, C. Wright. "The Mass Society." In *The Power Elite,* 298-324. New York: Oxford University Press, 2000.

Molina, Natalia. "Medicalizing the Mexican: Immigration, Race, and Disability in the Early-Twentieth-Century United States." *Radical History Review* 94, (December 2006):22-37. doi: 10.1215/01636545-2006-94-22.

National Center for Children in Poverty (NCCP). (2014). [Data File]. http://www.nccp.org

National Resource Center for Children and Families of the Incarcerated (NRCCFI). (2016). [Data File]. https://nrccfi.camden.rutgers.edu

NewsJunkiePost. "1/3rd of Women in US Military Raped." February 29, 2012. http://newsjunkiepost.com/2010/01/26/13rd-of-women-in-us-military-raped/

Olivera, Oscar and Lewis, Tom. *¡Cochabamba!: Water War in Bolivia.* New York: South End Press. 2004.

Page, Marianne. "Are Jobs the Solution to Poverty?" *Pathways: A Magazine on Poverty, Inequality, and Social Policy*, (Sept 2014): 9-13. https://inequality.stanford.edu/sites/default

Pauwels, Jacques R. *The Myth of the Good War: America in the Second World War.* Toronto:James Lorimer & Company, Ltd. 2009.

Pilisuk, Mark. and Hillier Parks, Susan. *The Healing Web: Social Networks and Human Survival.* Hanover:University Press of New England. 1986.

Piven, Frances. and Cloward,Richard. *Regulating the Poor: The Functions of Public Welfare.* New York:Vintage Books. 1993.

Phillips, Peter. *Giants: The Global Power Elite.* New York:Seven Stories Press. 2018.

Phillips, Peter and Huff, Mickey. "Inside the Military Media Industrial Complex: Impacts on Movements for Peace and Social Justice." *Dissident Voice*, December 22, 2009. https://constantinereport.com/inside-the-military-media-industrial-complex-impacts-on-movements-for-peace-and-social-justice/

Rank, Mark R., and Thomas A. Hirschl. "Rags or Riches? Estimating the Probabilities of Poverty and Affluence across the Adult American Life Span." *Social Science Quarterly* 82, no. 4 (2001): 651-69. http://www.jstor.org/stable/42955750.

Regional Economic Analysis Profile (REAP). San Francisco bay area economic submarket:Lake, Napa, and Sonoma counties. [Data File]. (2015). http://www.labormarketinfo.edd.ca.gov/Publications/REA-Reports/Lake-Napa-Sonoma-SFBay-REAP2015.pdf

Reiman, Jeffrey. *The Rich Get Richer and the Poor Get Prison Ideology, Class, and Criminal Justice.* Boston:Allyn and Bacon. 1998.

Rhodes, Richard. *The Making of the Atomic Bomb.* New York:Simon & Schuster Paperbacks.1986.

Robinson, James W. "American Poverty Cause Beliefs and Structured Inequality Legitimation." *Sociological Spectrum* 29, no. 4 (July 2009): 489-518. doi: 10.1080/02732170902904681.

RTQuestionMore. "Senate Refuses Abortion Rights for Rape Victims in the Military." https://www.rt.com/usa/women-military-rape-abortion-465/

Rutgers University. "Children and Families of the Incarcerated Fact Sheet." [Data File]. (2014). https://nrccfi.camden.rutgers.edu/files/nrccfi-fact-sheet-2014.pdf

Sadker, Myra and David Sadker. "Missing in Interaction." In *The Social Construction of Difference & Inequality: Race, Class, Gender and Sexuality*, edited by Tracy E. Ore, 305-317. New York: McGraw Hill. 1994.

Shipler, David K. *The Working Poor: Invisible in America*. New York: Vintage Books. 2005.

Stockdill, Brett C. "Forging a Multidimensional Oppositional Consciousness: Lessons from Community-Based AIDS Activism." In *Oppositional Consciousness: The Subjective Roots of Social Protest* edited by Jane Mansbridge and Aldon Morris, 204-237. Chicago:The University of Chicago Press. 2001.

Spier, Jackie. "Rapes of Women in Military 'a National Disgrace.'" SFGate. 02/29/2012. https://www.sfgate.com/opinion/article/Rapes-of-women-in-military-a-national-disgrace-2374845.php

Temple, Kathryn. "Exporting Violence: The School of the Americas, US Intervention in Latin America, and Resistance." (2007). No longer available.

Thomson, Rosemarie Garland. "Feminist Theory, the Body, and the Disabled Figure." In *Women's Lives: Multicultural Perspectives*, edited by Gwyn Kirk and Margo Okazawa-Rey. (156-163). New York:McGraw-Hill, 2007.

UN General Assembly, International Bill of Human Rights, 10 December 1948, A/RES/217(III)A-E, https://www.refworld.org/docid/3b00f08b48.html

UN General Assembly, International Covenant on Civil and Political Rights, 16 December 1966, United Nations, Treaty Series, vol. 999, p. 171, https://www.refworld.org/docid/3ae6b3aa0.html

UN General Assembly, International Covenant on Economic, Social and Cultural Rights, 16 December 1966, United Nations, Treaty Series, vol. 993, p. 3, https://www.refworld.org/docid/3ae6b36c0.html

UN General Assembly, "Universal Declaration of Human Rights," 217 (III) A (Paris, 1948), http://www.un.org/en/universal-declaration-human-rights/ *U.S. Constitution*. Preamble., Amend. I.

Wray, Matt. "'Three Generations of Imbeciles are Enough': American Eugenics and Poor White Trash." In *Not Quite White: White Trash and the Boundaries of Whiteness,* 65-95. Durham: Duke University Press, 2006.

Discussion Questions

PERSONAL IMPACT:

1) How is privilege and/or oppression part of your lived experience?

2) What are power dynamics and why do they matter?

3) Where would you place yourself within the current power structures, in terms of:

> Socioeconomic class, status, race, gender, religion, ethnicity, sexual orientation, age, ability, etc.?

4) What evidence of power dynamics have you observed or experienced?

> As a child? In your adult relationships? With co-workers, employers, friends? Consider all your relationships in your macro and micro environments.

5) What does structural inequality mean to you?

6) What words, attitudes, perceptions, prejudices, etc. have you observed or experienced?

> How does it affect you personally? Your loved ones? Co-workers? Etc.?

CULTURAL/SOCIAL:

7) What are some collective truths Americans have been manipulated to believe? Regarding:

> History, Masculinity, Femininity, Whiteness, Blackness, Sexuality, Beauty Ideals, Normative Behaviors, Otherness.

8) How does the social system of Patriarchy create and maintain structural inequalities?

9) How embedded is the culture of domination and violence? Consider macro and micro level dynamics.

ECONOMICS:

10) How does the economic system of Capitalism create and maintain structural inequalities?

11) How is the public manipulated for Consumerism, Conformance, Commodification, and Consumption?

12) What crises have been created by Capitalism or capitalist goals?

POLITICAL:

13) How does the political system of Democracy (in its current state) create and maintain structural inequalities?

14) Is the American public consciousness being manipulated by a Power Elite? In what ways? By what methods?

15) Is the United States an Imperialist nation? How does this contribute to foreign policy?

OPPORTUNITIES FOR CHANGE:

16) How can we start restructuring for Interdependence? What would this look like?

17) How do we begin breaking down barriers and building alliances? Where do previously marginalized voices fit in to constructing relationships based on mutual respect and appreciation for diversity?

18) Can common ground be found? Can we, as individuals open our hearts and minds enough to consider the greater good for all?

About the Author

Julie Banks Lewis is an activist, speaker, and author focusing on universal human rights and economic social justice. With her book *Critical Masses: Who Wins, Who Loses, Who Decides*, Lewis explores how power dynamics are manipulated and structural inequalities created and maintained for the privileging of a relatively few and the oppression of many. Further, she examines how each of us is implicated in current power relations and how we may think, feel, and act to change them.

Her unique perspectives have been molded by her experiential knowledge as an economically challenged, single mother of three children, an other-abled individual, and as an adult survivor of sexual, physical, and emotional childhood abuse. She attended Sonoma State University where she earned a BA in Women's and Gender Studies (WGS) and an MA in a self-designed Interdisciplinary Studies program: Power Dynamics and Structural Inequalities. She is an organic intellectual, deconstructing official historical and cultural narratives, and marrying theoretical explanations with real-life experience. Her goals are to compel hearts, challenge minds, and connect lives in an earnest attempt to upset the status quo and help create understanding for a social order that elevates all peoples and subjugates none.

When not seeking out ways in which to change the world, bring peace among all peoples, and save the planet—she spends time enjoying nature in beautiful Colorado with her preteen daughter, her two adult daughters, their husbands, and her young grandson.